USING

microsoft®

project

2010

Sonia Atchison and Brian Kennemer

800 East 96th Street, Indianapolis, Indiana 46240 USA

Using Microsoft® Project 2010

Copyright © 2011 by Pearson Education, Inc.

ISBN-13: 978-0-7897-4295-7

ISBN-10: 0-7897-4295-0

The Library of Congress Cataloging-in-Publication Data is on file.

Printed in the United States of America

First Printing: April 2011

Trademarks

All terms mentioned in this book that are known to be trademarks or service marks have been appropriately capitalized. Que Publishing cannot attest to the accuracy of this information. Use of a term in this book should not be regarded as affecting the validity of any trademark or service mark.

Warning and Disclaimer

Every effort has been made to make this book as complete and as accurate as possible, but no warranty or fitness is implied. The information provided is on an "as is" basis. The authors and the publisher shall have neither liability nor responsibility to any person or entity with respect to any loss or damages arising from the information contained in this book or from the use of the programs accompanying it.

Bulk Sales

Que Publishing offers excellent discounts on this book when ordered in quantity for bulk purchases or special sales. For more information, please contact

U.S. Corporate and Government Sales
1-800-382-3419
corpsales@pearsontechgroup.com

For sales outside of the United States, please contact

International Sales
international@pearson.com

Associate Publisher
Greg Wiegand

Acquisitions Editor
Loretta Yates

Development Editor
Abshier House

Managing Editor
Kristy Hart

Project Editor
Jovana San Nicolas-Shirley

Copy Editor
Bart Reed

Indexer
Lisa Stumpf

Proofreader
Sheri Cain

Technical Editor
Brian Kennemer

Publishing Coordinator
Cindy Teeters

Interior Designer
Anne Jones

Cover Designer
Anna Stingley

Compositor
Nonie Ratcliff

Contents at a Glance

Media Table of Contents

To register this product and gain access to the Free Web Edition and the audio and video files, go to quepublishing.com/using.

Table of Contents

About the Authors

Sonia Atchison has been working with Microsoft Project since 1999. In 2006, she joined the writing team at Microsoft that produces end-user Help content and videos for Project and Project Server, planning and writing content for the 2007 and 2010 releases.

Brian Kennemer has been helping people understand and work with Microsoft Project since 1998. He has worked at Microsoft, where he specialized in Project Server deployments and was a member of the Enterprise Project Management Center of Excellence. He currently does Project Server consulting at forProject Technology, Inc., a Microsoft partner that specializes in Earned Value Management System products that work with Project and Project Server. He lives in the forests north of Seattle with his wife, Alicia, and his children, Riley, Jesse, and Alivia.

Acknowledgments

For their unending patience, thanks to Vince Atchison, Jasper Atchison, Brian Kennemer, and Loretta Yates.

—Sonia Atchison

My thanks go to my wife Alicia and my children Riley, Jesse, and Alivia for their support that allowed me to work on this book. Thanks also to Sonia Atchison and Loretta Yates.

—Brian Kennemer

We Want to Hear from You!

As the reader of this book, *you* are our most important critic and commentator. We value your opinion and want to know what we're doing right, what we could do better, what areas you'd like to see us publish in, and any other words of wisdom you're willing to pass our way.

As an associate publisher for Que Publishing, I welcome your comments. You can email or write me directly to let me know what you did or didn't like about this book—as well as what we can do to make our books better.

Please note that I cannot help you with technical problems related to the topic of this book. We do have a User Services group, however, where I will forward specific technical questions related to the book.

When you write, please be sure to include this book's title and author as well as your name, email address, and phone number. I will carefully review your comments and share them with the author and editors who worked on the book.

Email: feedback@quepublishing.com

Mail: Greg Wiegand
         Associate Publisher
         Que Publishing
         800 East 96th Street
         Indianapolis, IN 46240 USA

Reader Services

Visit our website and register this book at quepublishing.com/using for convenient access to any updates, downloads, or errata that might be available for this book.

Introduction

Project management is a broad term that can mean something very formal and specific to one person, but something very organic and pieced together to another. The fact of the matter is that "pieced together" can get you only so far. Spreadsheets, sticky notes, and email are all great tools, and they may work fine for smaller projects, but when you start adding just a few more people working on a project, or just one or two more reports to generate for upper management, project management becomes more complicated. Your blood pressure goes up a smidge and gathering bits and pieces from the various tools you've been using to track your projects gets to be more tedious than you may have time for.

Microsoft Project 2010 addresses these issues gracefully and powerfully. I can't lie; it has a steep learning curve, but it's absolutely worth your time to figure it out, even at a rudimentary level. The amount of time it ultimately will save you is reason enough. And as you complete projects, you can review the project data to help make decisions about future projects. It's a thing of beauty, really, especially if you've been used to a lot of manual updating and high-maintenance project and resource tracking.

Project 2010 is versatile enough to help bring order to a novice project manager's plans, while offering rich solutions for experienced project managers. The latter will benefit from items such as earned value and critical path analysis, resource leveling, and heavy customizability to meet organizational needs.

How This Book Is Organized

This book introduces you to Project 2010. It is designed to familiarize you with project management terminology, as it is used in Project 2010, and covers functionality that was brought forward from previous versions of Project, as well as features that are new in Project 2010. This book is far from a be-all, end-all reference book for Project 2010. Instead, it focuses on introducing the concepts and procedures that are most commonly used. *Using Microsoft Project 2010* offers you the following:

- Some high-level project management theory, as it applies to Project 2010

- An introduction to new features in this version

- An orientation to Project 2010, including the different parts of the Project window and the many views available to you

- A walkthrough of the process of creating a project, from adding tasks and assigning resources, to tracking costs and reporting on progress

- Information about some simple customization options, as a starting point for more advanced topics

- Some solutions to commonly encountered project issues

Using This Book

This book allows you to customize your own learning experience. The step-by-step instructions in this book give you a solid foundation in using Project 2010, while rich and varied online content, including video tutorials and audio sidebars, provide the following:

- Demonstrations of step-by-step tasks covered in this book

- Additional tips or information on a topic

- Practical advice and suggestions

- Direction for more advanced tasks not covered in this book

Here's a quick look at a few structural features designed to help you get the most out of this book:

- **Chapter objective**—At the beginning of each chapter is a brief summary of topics addressed in that chapter. This objective enables you to quickly see what is covered in the chapter.

- **Notes**—Notes provide additional commentary or explanation that doesn't fit neatly into the surrounding text. Notes give detailed explanations of how something works, alternative ways of performing a task, and other tidbits to get you on your way.

- **Tips**—This element gives you shortcuts, workarounds, and ways to avoid pitfalls.

- **Cautions**—Every once in a while, there is something that can have serious repercussions if done incorrectly (or rarely, if done at all). Cautions give you a heads-up.

- **Cross-references**—Many topics are connected to other topics in various ways. Cross-references help you link related information together, no matter where that information appears in the book. When another section is related to one you are reading, a cross-reference directs you to a specific page in the book on which you can find the related information.

 LET ME TRY IT tasks are presented in a step-by-step sequence so you can easily follow along.

 SHOW ME video walks through tasks you've just got to see—including bonus advanced techniques.

 TELL ME MORE audio delivers practical insights straight from the experts.

Special Features

More than just a book, your *Using* product integrates step-by-step video tutorials and valuable audio sidebars delivered through the **Free Web Edition** that comes with every *Using* book. For the price of this book, you get online access anywhere with a web connection—no books to carry, content is updated as the technology changes, and the benefit of video and audio learning.

About the *Using* Web Edition

The Web Edition of every *Using* book is powered by **Safari Books Online**, allowing you to access the video tutorials and valuable audio sidebars. Plus, you can search the contents of the book, highlight text and attach a note to that text, print your notes and highlights in a custom summary, and cut and paste directly from Safari Books Online.

To register this product and gain access to the free Web Edition and the audio and video files, go to **quepublishing.com/using**.

This chapter provides a basic understanding of project management terminology, Microsoft Project 2010, and what's new in this version.

1

Introduction to Managing Projects with Microsoft Project 2010

Here's a common scenario: You've been put in charge of some project in your organization. This project requires scheduling, coordinating, and progress tracking. Your office is covered in yellow sticky notes, and you have five different spreadsheets going at once, which each need to be updated manually every time a date changes. Your manager is knocking at your office door, asking for a status report for a meeting she has in 10 minutes, and you're feeling panicky because you don't even know where to start to pull together a summary of what's going on with your project, let alone what that summary is going to reveal about the project's status.

This is the point at which you, as a project manager, can either throw your hands up and find a new line of work or step up to the plate and take your project management skills to the next level. What's the next level? Tools. My recommendation? Microsoft Project 2010, for its powerful scheduling engine and customizability.

What Microsoft Project 2010 Can Do for You

Microsoft Project 2010 is a software tool that takes a lot of the manual updating and guesswork out of managing your projects. You can enter information about your project's tasks, when they need to happen, how long you think they should take, and who should be doing the work. As you make updates, Project 2010's scheduling engine takes all the project work into account, providing a grounded schedule that represents the reality of what can be accomplished. After you've seen the facts, you can move forward and make adjustments to the time, scope, or costs involved with your project, to find acceptable solutions for time-management challenges.

If you're not sure how to adjust your project to meet certain constraints, consider the project management triangle: one side each for time, scope, and costs associated with your project. Figure 1.1 illustrates this triangle. If you have fewer people working on the project than you had planned, you'll need to make up for that by extending the project deadline or limiting the scope of your project. If you have a smaller budget than planned, you'll need to adjust your project by not doing quite as much work or completing the work in less time. If your project expands to include more work, you'll need to increase the budget to hire more people or extend the schedule so that the people currently assigned to the project have more time to finish the added work.

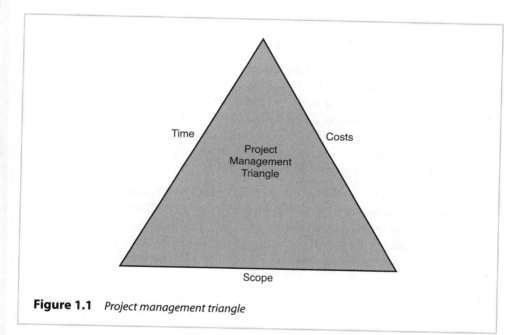

Figure 1.1 *Project management triangle*

As work progresses, you can track how close the actual schedule is to your original baseline dates, so that you can more accurately predict when your project may be completed. If you need to be done sooner, you can use Project 2010 to model what would happen if you added more people to ease the workload or increased the project's budget to allow the current set of people working on the project to spend even more time getting the work done. Or if you need to pull some people off of your project, you can use Project 2010 to model what your project's dates will look like with fewer people doing the work.

As in the earlier scenario, when your manager knocks on your door asking for a status report in the next 10 minutes, you can use the reporting features in Project 2010 to quickly produce any of several attractive reports, showing things such as overall project health, budget tracking, and earned value over time. And you'll already know what the reports will reveal, because each time you make changes, the charts and views that illustrate your project's work over the course of the schedule are updated in real time. No surprises!

SHOW ME   Media 1.1—What Is Project 2010?
Access this video file through your registered Web Edition at
my.safaribooksonline.com/9780132182461/media.

What Version of Project 2010 Do You Need?

The two versions of Project 2010 are Standard and Professional. For many people, Project Standard 2010 has all the functionality they need. However, if you find that you do a lot of reassigning of staff or shifting of the tools you need to get work done, Project Professional 2010 has more advanced features to help you get the right people doing the right tasks. Project Professional 2010 also has advanced functionality to help you share your plan with others, using Microsoft SharePoint Foundation 2010 or Microsoft Project Server 2010.

If you're looking for an end-to-end enterprise project management solution, you can use Project Professional 2010 with Project Server 2010. With both of these tools deployed in your organization, people can submit project proposals for analysis by stakeholders, project managers can plan and track work in either a desktop client or on the Web, and team members can report time and task progress using Project Web App.

An end-to-end enterprise project management solution can be beneficial for small organizations as well as for medium and large organizations. If you choose to evaluate this option, keep in mind that the functionality offered in this solution can be scaled up or down to meet your organization's needs.

TELL ME MORE   Media 1.2—What Version of Project Is Right for Me?
Access this audio recording through your registered Web Edition at
my.safaribooksonline.com/9780132182461/media.

Laying a Foundation

Before we talk about the details of using Project 2010, you need to clearly understand a few terms, because they're used extensively in the Project 2010 interface.

SHOW ME   Media 1.3—Project Terminology
Access this video file through your registered Web Edition at
my.safaribooksonline.com/9780132182461/media.

Project

Just so we're clear, in relation to Project 2010, a *project* is a set of work that is completed according to a schedule and that has some kind of end result. For example, a project may result in a tangible item, such as a report, a building, or a retail product, or it may result in an intangible item, such as an event, a set of goals, or a strategy.

Task

A *task* is a smaller chunk of work that contributes to the completion of a project. For example, if you're planning a project to build a house, you might have separate tasks for laying the foundation, putting up the walls, and adding the roof. In Project 2010, each task has a start date and a finish date, and you can assign people and/or things to help do the task work.

Resource

A *resource* can be a person, an item, a facility, or an expense that is required to complete the work associated with a task. In Project 2010, people are referred to as *work* resources; items or facilities are referred to as *material* resources; and expenses are referred to as *cost* resources. A single task may require more than one type of resource. For example, if the task is to travel to a satellite office and teach a training course, you might need a person (work resource) to teach the class, a roundtrip plane ticket (cost resource) to get the person to and from the satellite office, and a classroom (material resource) where the training course is held.

Assignment

An *assignment* is the term used when a resource is identified as a person, item, or cost that will do work on, or be used for, a task in a project.

What's New in Project 2010?

The following sections provide a high-level overview of what's been updated or added in Project 2010.

Updated User Interface

The most noticeable change in Project 2010 is the addition of the *ribbon*. If you used the 2007 version of Access, Excel, PowerPoint, or Word, you may be familiar with the ribbon. Commands that previously had been available in the menus at the top of the Project window are now available as buttons on several tabs across the top of each view, as shown in Figure 1.2.

Figure 1.2   *The ribbon is displayed at the top of the Project window.*

As you work in Project 2010, the tabs display commonly used commands for whatever you happen to be doing. For example, if you're making changes to the way the Gantt Chart view is displayed, there's an entire tab with buttons that control what bars are displayed, what colors are used, and other formatting options.

The ribbon takes up a good amount of real estate in the Project 2010 window. If you find yourself needing just a little more room to display your project, press Ctrl+F1 to minimize the ribbon. When the ribbon is minimized, only the tab names appear at the top of the window. When you click a tab name, the ribbon appears. When you click outside the ribbon, it goes back to being minimized. Press Ctrl+F1 again to bring the ribbon back.

SHOW ME   Media 1.4—Introducing the Ribbon
Access this video file through your registered Web Edition at
my.safaribooksonline.com/9780132182461/media.

LET ME TRY IT

Using the Ribbon

To get familiar with using the ribbon, follow these steps:

1. Click through the tabs on the ribbon to get familiar with the buttons and options available on each tab.

2. Press **Ctrl+F1** to minimize the ribbon. Click a tab on the minimized ribbon to display the full ribbon, and then click outside of the ribbon to return the tabs to minimized. Press **Ctrl+F1** again to maximize the ribbon.

Manually Scheduled Tasks

In previous versions of Project, tasks could be scheduled only using Project's scheduling engine. That is, you'd tell Project a few details about a task, such as when it should start and how long it should take (duration), and Project would figure out when the task would be done, based on how many people or things were assigned to the task, what other things the task depended on, and what the calendar looked like. Until you had a good understanding of how Project was making these calculations, the scheduling engine seemed to be a bit of a mystery. Even some experienced project managers who had been using Project for years occasionally would run into situations in complex projects in which the dates given by the scheduling engine were just not what they expected.

Project 2010 has taken a new approach to scheduling by introducing *manually scheduled tasks*. That is, instead of letting Project 2010 calculate when a project should start or finish, you can identify a task as being manually scheduled, and then you have full control over task start and finish dates.

 SHOW ME   Media 1.5—A Look at Manually Scheduled Tasks
Access this video file through your registered Web Edition at
my.safaribooksonline.com/9780132182461/media.

As you might guess, choosing to manually schedule a task can be a blessing and a curse. On the one hand, your dates are firm, and you won't be stuck sitting there trying to figure out why the task start date is a week later than you thought it should be. On the other hand, by forcing a task to start and finish on specific dates, you may forget to account for company holidays, the people working on your task are more likely to have too much work on their plates, and you may end up accidentally double-booking tools or facilities required to get the work done. If you choose to manually schedule a task, you'll need to keep a close eye on how that task is affected by the rest of your project and what impact that task may have on other tasks and resources.

Team Planner View

The Team Planner view, available only in Project Professional 2010, is a quick, easy, and highly visual way to review and change what your team members are working on in your project. In the Team Planner view, shown in Figure 1.3, you can see where people may have too much on their plates (overallocation), what tasks have yet to be assigned, and what the current progress is on your project's tasks.

The darkened portion of this task shows how much work has progressed.

The red highlighting shows where this resource is overallocated.

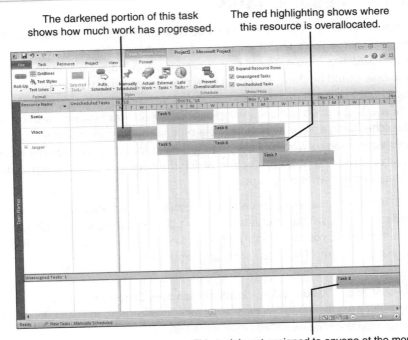

This task is not assigned to anyone at the moment. Drag it to a resource name above to assign it.

Figure 1.3   *The Team Planner view shows what each team member is working on.*

You can resolve overallocations by dragging tasks between team members and assign tasks to people by dragging them from the Unassigned Tasks area of this view to a team member's name.

SHOW ME   Media 1.6—An Overview of the Team Planner View
Access this video file through your registered Web Edition at
my.safaribooksonline.com/9780132182461/media.

Timeline

At the top of each view, you can display a *timeline* of your project, illustrating project tasks and dates (see Figure 1.4).

You can use the timeline to help focus what's displayed in other Project views. This timeline can be printed or copied and pasted into other applications, enabling you

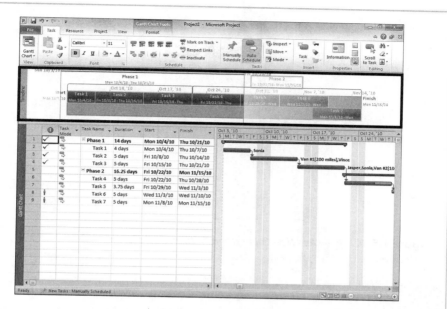

Figure 1.4   *The timeline can be displayed above another view.*

to easily communicate your project plan with others who don't have access to your plan or don't have Project 2010 installed.

SHOW ME   Media 1.7—Advantages of the Timeline
Access this video file through your registered Web Edition at
my.safaribooksonline.com/9780132182461/media.

New Table Customization

Adding new columns to any of the tables in Project 2010 is considerably easier than in prior versions. Instead of going through a separate window and several customization steps, you now can simply click the **Add New Column** header on the right side of any table, as shown in Figure 1.5.

When you click the **Add New Column** header, the entire list of available fields is displayed for you to choose which column you want to add. After the column is added, you can drag it to where you want it displayed. If you decide you need to rename a column, you can simply double-click the column header and type the new name. So easy!

Figure 1.5   *Click the Add New Column header to insert a new column.*

SHOW ME   1.8—Adding a New Column
Access this video file through your registered Web Edition at
my.safaribooksonline.com/9780132182461/media.

LET ME TRY IT

Adding a New Column to a View

To add a new column to a view, follow these steps:

1. Click the **Add New Column** header, and then click the name of a column you want to add to the current view.

2. Click the column header for the new column. The cursor turns to a four-way arrow. Click and drag the header to move it to another location in the view.

3. To rename the column, double-click the column header and type a new name.

SharePoint Collaboration

If you have Project Professional 2010, you can export your project to a SharePoint project tasks list, which is included as part of SharePoint Foundation 2010. This enables you to share project information without Project Server 2010 and without requiring others to have Project 2010 installed. Figure 1.6 shows the Sync with Tasks List options on the File tab.

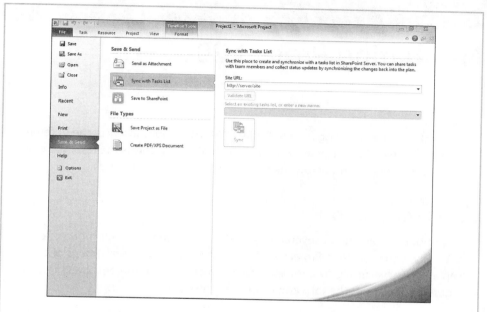

Figure 1.6   *The File tab includes multiple options for working with SharePoint.*

In this chapter, you'll learn how to navigate around the interface and how to use the views in Project 2010.

2

Navigating Project 2010

The first step in really digging into Project 2010 is to look closely at the different parts of the user interface. At the top of the Project window is the ribbon, below that is the timeline, and below the timeline is the view display area.

Using the Ribbon

The ribbon is made up of several *tabs* that display commands appropriate for whatever view you're using in Project 2010. Each tab contains several *groups* of buttons, separated by vertical gray lines and labeled in gray text at the bottom of the tab. Figure 2.1 illustrates the tabs and groups on the ribbon.

Tabs

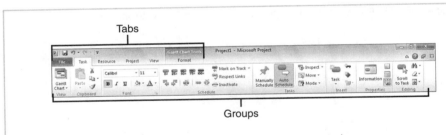

Groups

Figure 2.1   *The ribbon is displayed at the top of the Project window.*

The Task, Resource, Project, and View tabs are always available, with some buttons on each tab made unavailable depending on what view you're using or what you have selected.

Each view in Project 2010 has a special Format tab with buttons for commands that you can only use in each view. This special tab is the last one on the right and is highlighted using a different color for each view.

If you're familiar with previous versions of Project, you may find the interactive ribbon mapping guides available on Office.com helpful in learning where to find menu commands on the ribbon. To view the Project 2010 interactive guide, go to http://office.microsoft.com/en-us/project-help/learn-where-menu-and-toolbar-commands-are-in-office-2010-HA101794130.aspx and then click **Open the Project guide**, under **Use an interactive guide to find my commands**.

A printable guide is also available on this page, if you'd prefer a desk reference.

For more information on using the ribbon, see Show Me Media 1.3.

Using the Timeline

The timeline, which illustrates your project's tasks, is displayed between the ribbon and the main viewing area in the Project 2010 window. The timeline can be very helpful in communicating your project data with others.

Where'd the timeline go? The timeline can be turned on or off at any time. On the ribbon, click the **View** tab and then select or clear the **Timeline** box in the **Split View** group to turn the timeline on or off.

If you click within the timeline portion of the window, a Format tab specific to the timeline is displayed on the ribbon, in the shaded area labeled Timeline Tools (shown in Figure 2.2).

Figure 2.2   *The Format tab for the timeline contains several view options.*

You can use the buttons on the Format tab for the timeline to add tasks and milestones to the timeline, change the date formats used for each task on the timeline, and change the text styles used for different elements of the timeline. Tasks can be displayed as bars within the timeline, or as callouts above or below the timeline.

After you have the timeline displayed with the information you want, you can share it with others.

SHOW ME   Media 2.1—Sharing the Timeline
Access this video file through your registered Web Edition at
my.safaribooksonline.com/9780132182461/media.

LET ME TRY IT

Share the Timeline with Others

To share the Timeline with others, follow these steps:

1. On the **Format** tab, in the **Copy** group, click **Copy Timeline**.

2. Choose whether you want to copy the Timeline **For E-mail**, **For Presentation**, or **Full Size**. The timeline is copied to your clipboard.

3. Paste the Timeline in another application, such as Outlook, Word, or PowerPoint, for sharing with others.

Understanding Project Views

Project 2010 has 27 built-in views that you can use to see different information about your project. Views display *task* information, such as task names and dates, *resource* information, such as names and rates for the people involved with your project, and *assignment* information, such as what tasks a specific person is working on at a given time.

SHOW ME   Media 2.2—Understanding Project Views
Access this video file through your registered Web Edition at
my.safaribooksonline.com/9780132182461/media.

What Views Are Available in Project 2010?

Project 2010 provides several different default views, each designed for a unique purpose. The following sections go over each default view.

TELL ME MORE   Media 2.3—Deciding Which View You Should Use
Access this audio recording through your registered Web Edition at
my.safaribooksonline.com/9780132182461/media.

Bar Rollup

Use the Bar Rollup view, shown in Figure 2.3, to display subtasks overlapping summary tasks on the Gantt Chart.

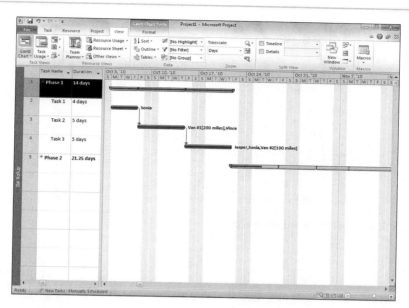

Figure 2.3 *The Bar Rollup view*

  LET ME TRY IT

Roll Up a Subtask

To include a subtask overlapped on a summary task in the Bar Rollup view, follow these steps:

1. In the **Bar Rollup** view, double-click a subtask to display the **Task Information** dialog box.

2. On the **General** tab, select the **Rollup** check box, shown in Figure 2.4.

3. Click **OK**. The subtask bar now appears overlapped on its summary task bar on the Gantt chart.

Calendar

The Calendar view, shown in Figure 2.5, displays your project's tasks as overlays in a standard calendar format. This view enables you to jump between viewing a month, a week, or a custom span of weeks or dates.

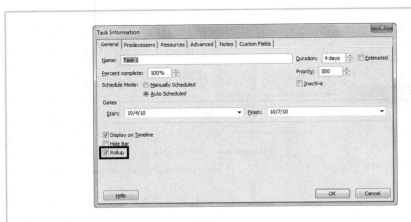

Figure 2.4   *Select the Rollup check box.*

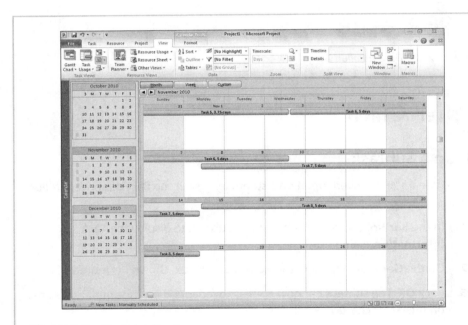

Figure 2.5   *The Calendar view*

Click **Month**, **Week**, or **Custom**, above the calendar, to change what dates the Calendar view displays. Figure 2.6 highlights these buttons on the Calendar view.

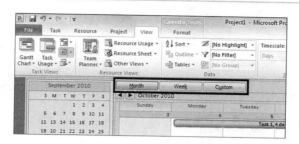

Figure 2.6   *Click Month, Week, or Custom.*

 LET ME TRY IT

Set a Custom Calendar Period

To choose a specific set of dates to display in the Calendar view, follow these steps:

1. In the **Calendar** view, click **Custom**, above the calendar.

2. On the **Zoom** dialog box, choose whether you want to display a certain number of weeks, or a specific date range, using the options shown in Figure 2.7.

3. Click **OK**. The calendar is updated to display the period you specified.

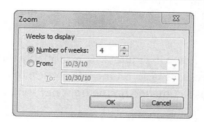

Figure 2.7   *Use the Zoom dialog box to set a custom calendar period.*

Descriptive Network Diagram

As shown in Figure 2.8, the Descriptive Network Diagram view displays boxes for each task in your project, containing details about each task. When appropriate, the boxes are connected using arrows that show dependencies between the tasks. Tasks on the critical path are highlighted in red.

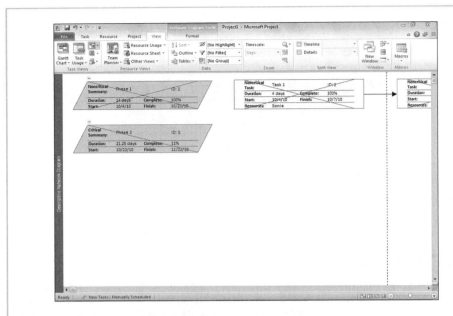

Figure 2.8   *The Descriptive Network Diagram view*

Detail Gantt

The Detail Gantt view, shown in Figure 2.9, helps to highlight how much a task can be delayed before other task dates are impacted. This view shows the critical path using red bars on the Gantt chart.

Gantt Chart

The Gantt Chart view, shown in Figure 2.10, is probably the most-used view in Project 2010. It lists the project's tasks on the left portion of the view, and displays coordinating bars across a timeline on the right portion of the view.

Gantt with Timeline

The Gantt with Timeline view, shown in Figure 2.11, is a split view that displays the Timeline view in the top pane and the Gantt Chart view in the bottom pane.

Leveling Gantt

The Leveling Gantt view, shown in Figure 2.12, shows how the tasks in your project will be affected if you use the resource-leveling feature in Project 2010.

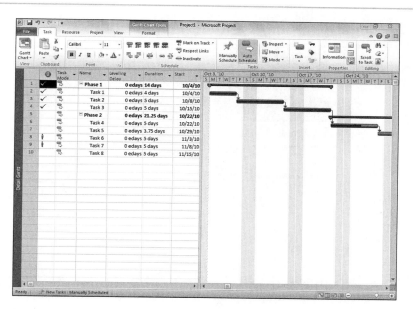

Figure 2.9   *The Detail Gantt view*

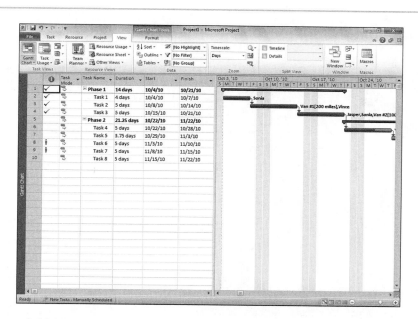

Figure 2.10   *The Gantt Chart view*

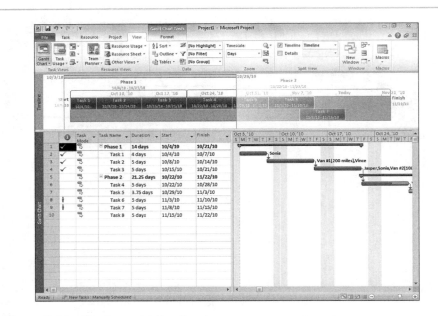

Figure 2.11 *The Gantt with Timeline view*

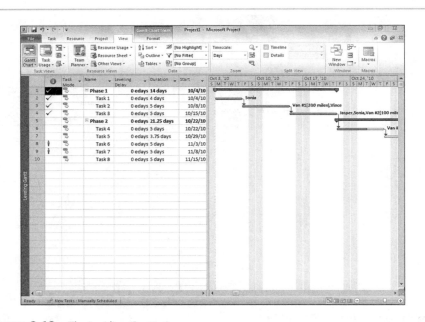

Figure 2.12 *The Leveling Gantt view*

Milestone Date Rollup

Use the Milestone Date Rollup view, shown in Figure 2.13, to view your project's summary tasks on the Gantt chart, with labels for milestones and dates.

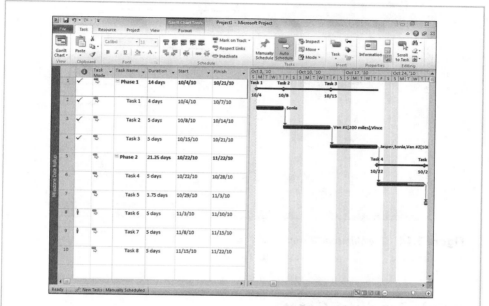

Figure 2.13   *The Milestone Date Rollup view*

The Milestone Date Rollup view will only display milestones and dates on the summary task Gantt bar if the subtasks are set to roll up to the summary task. Refer to the section, "Roll Up a Subtask," for information on how to roll subtasks up to the summary task level.

Milestone Rollup

Use the Milestone Rollup view, shown in Figure 2.14, to view your project's summary tasks on the Gantt chart, with labels for milestones.

The Milestone Rollup view will only display milestones on the summary task Gantt bar if the subtasks are set to roll up to the summary task. Refer to the section, "Roll Up a Subtask," for information on how to roll subtasks up to the summary task level.

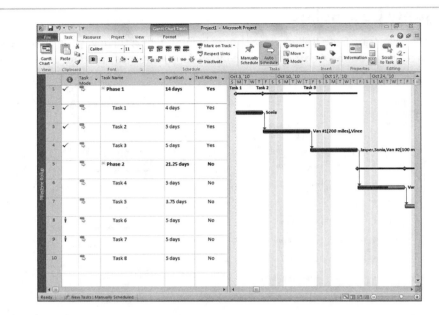

Figure 2.14   *The Milestone Rollup view*

Multiple Baselines Gantt

The Multiple Baselines Gantt view, shown in Figure 2.15, displays the dates saved as **Baseline**, **Baseline 1**, and **Baseline 2**, using different colored Gantt bars on the right portion of the view.

Network Diagram

The Network Diagram view, shown in Figure 2.16, displays boxes for each task in your project. When appropriate, the boxes are connected using arrows that show dependencies between the tasks. Tasks on the critical path are highlighted in red. This view may come in handy when you need an illustrated look at how tasks in your project are connected.

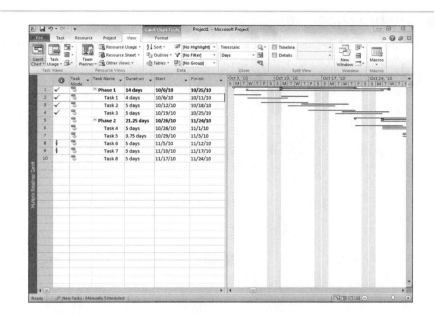

Figure 2.15   *The Multiple Baselines Gantt view*

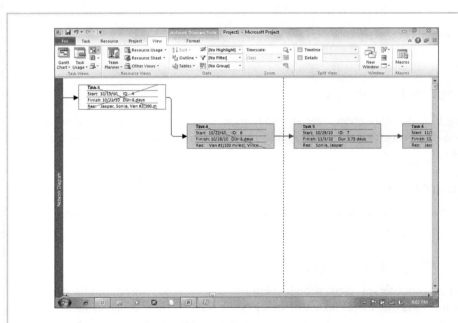

Figure 2.16   *The Network Diagram view*

Relationship Diagram

Use the **Relationship Diagram** view, shown in Figure 2.17, to clarify how a single task relates to other tasks, in projects with many dependencies.

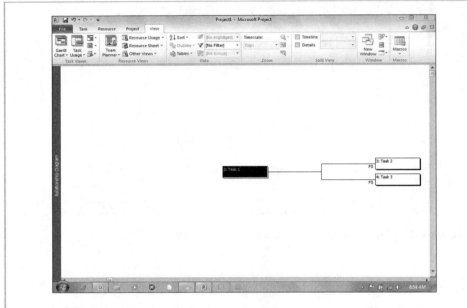

Figure 2.17   *The Relationship Diagram view*

Resource Allocation

The Resource Allocation view, shown in Figure 2.18, is a split view, displaying the Resource Usage view in the top pane and the Leveling Gantt view in the bottom pane.

Resource Form

The Resource Form view, shown in Figure 2.19 enables you to view or enter detailed information about each of your project's resources individually.

Resource Graph

The Resource Graph view, shown in Figure 2.20, displays a bar graph for each resource assigned to at least one task in your project. The bar graph illustrates allocation, availability, cost, and work details throughout the project's life cycle.

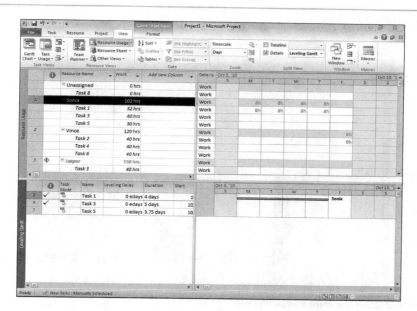

Figure 2.18   *The Resource Allocation view*

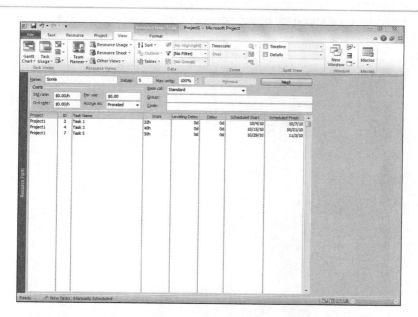

Figure 2.19   *The Resource Form view*

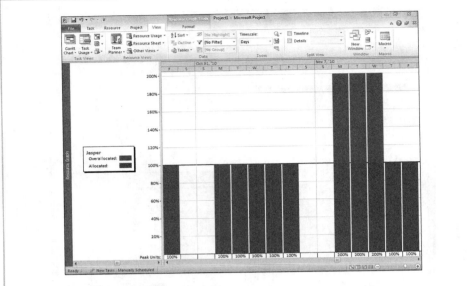

Figure 2.20   *The Resource Graph view*

Resource Name Form

The Resource Name Form view, shown in Figure 2.21, enables you to view or enter basic information about each of your project's resources individually.

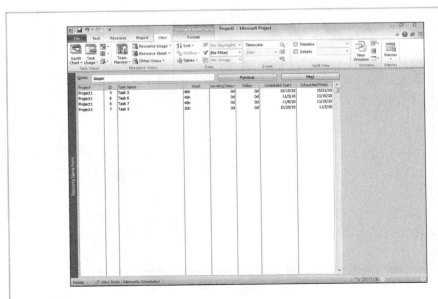

Figure 2.21   *The Resource Name Form view*

Resource Sheet

Use the Resource Sheet view, shown in Figure 2.22, to enter or review details about the resources that may be assigned to tasks in your project.

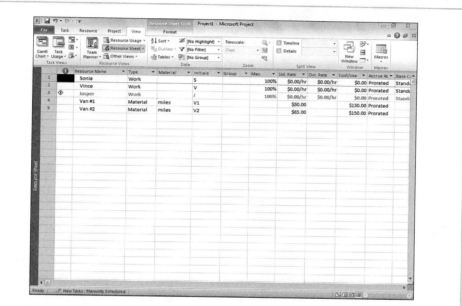

Figure 2.22   *The Resource Sheet view*

Resource Usage

The Resource Usage view, shown in Figure 2.23, displays task assignments for each resource on the left portion of the view, and the work or cost information about the task assignments over time in the right portion of the view.

Task Details Form

The Task Details Form view, shown in Figure 2.24, enables you to view or enter detailed information about each of your project's tasks individually.

Task Entry

The Task Entry view, shown in Figure 2.25, is a split view, displaying the Gantt Chart view in the top pane and the Task Form view in the bottom pane.

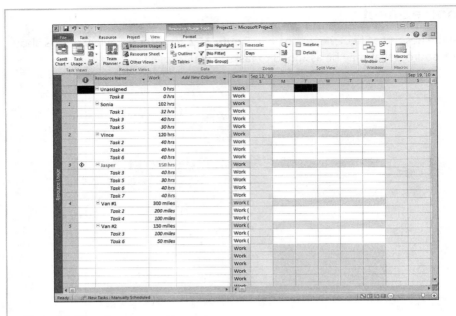

Figure 2.23   *The Resource Usage view*

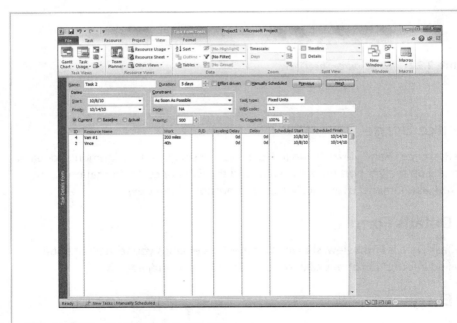

Figure 2.24   *The Task Details Form view*

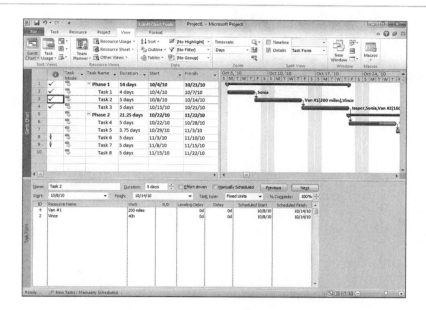

Figure 2.25   *The Task Entry view*

Task Form

The Task Form view, shown in Figure 2.26, enables you to view or enter basic information about each of your project's tasks individually.

Task Name Form

Use the Task Name Form view, shown in Figure 2.27, to view or enter a single task's assigned resources, predecessors, and successors.

Task Sheet

The Task Sheet view, shown in Figure 2.28, enables you to view or enter task information without simultaneously viewing the Gantt chart.

Task Usage

The Task Usage view, shown in Figure 2.29, displays assigned resources for each task on the left portion of the view, and the work or cost information about the resource assignments over time in the right portion of the view.

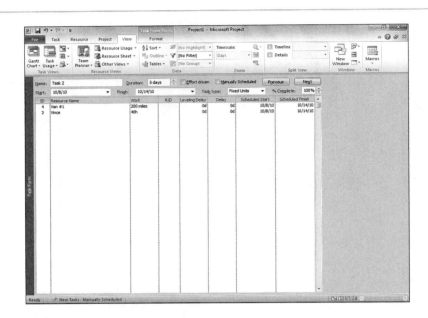

Figure 2.26   *The Task Form view*

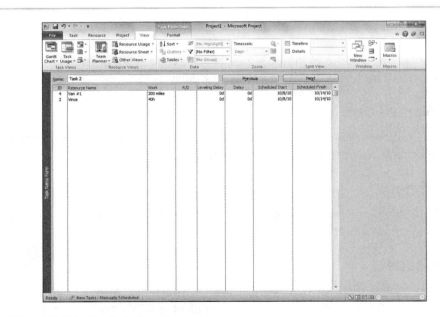

Figure 2.27   *The Task Name Form view*

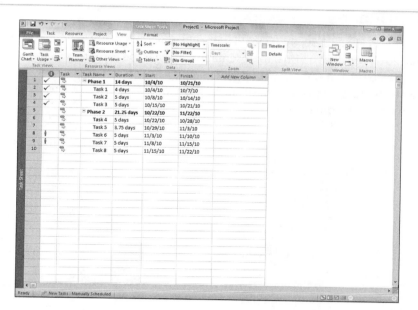

Figure 2.28   *The Task Sheet view*

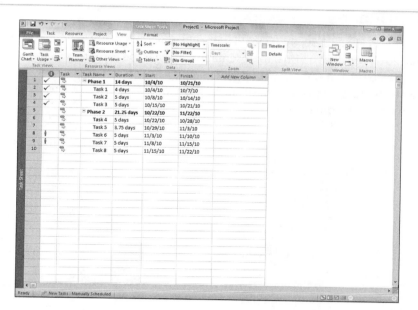

Figure 2.29   *The Task Usage view*

Team Planner

As shown in Figure 2.30, the Team Planner view, available only in Project Professional 2010, provides a visual representation of what the resources in your project are working on, throughout your project's life cycle. You can drag task assignments between resources to adjust for overallocation or free up some of a resource's time to make room for other work.

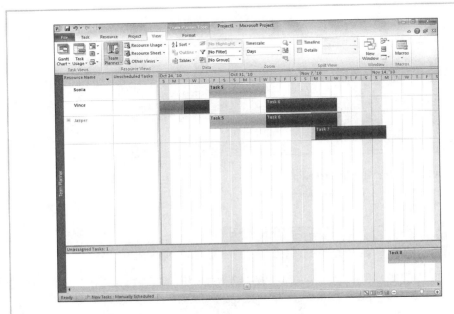

Figure 2.30   *The Team Planner view*

Timeline

The Timeline view, shown in Figure 2.31, illustrates your project's tasks and dates using a traditional timeline format. It can be customized to display certain tasks as callouts on the timeline, and it can be printed or copied into other applications.

Tracking Gantt

The Tracking Gantt view, shown in Figure 2.32, displays Gantt bars for the baseline dates and the current schedule for each of your project's tasks. This enables you to quickly see how well your project is tracking to your baseline dates.

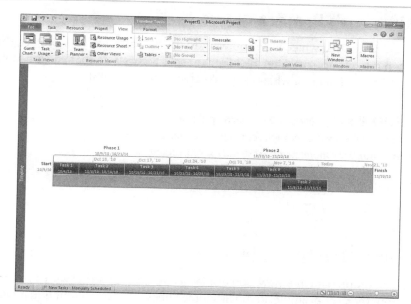

Figure 2.31   *The Timeline view*

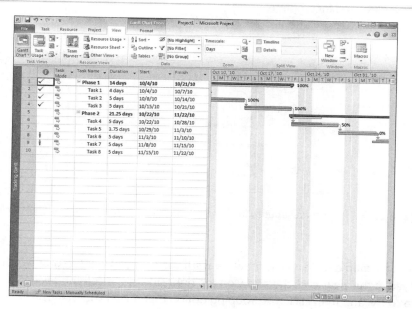

Figure 2.32   *The Tracking Gantt view*

Working with Project Views

After you've decided which view you want to use to work with your project, the next step is to group, sort, filter, highlight, or split the view so that you are looking at the right set of data for whatever you're trying to accomplish.

 SHOW ME   Media 2.4—Group Data in a View
Access this video file through your registered Web Edition at
my.safaribooksonline.com/9780132182461/media.

 LET ME TRY IT

Grouping Data in a View

When you group data in a view, you display all tasks or resources with a common factor together. For example, in the Resource Sheet view, you might find it helpful to group the resources by Type, so that all work resources are displayed together, all material resources are displayed together, and all cost resources are displayed together. Figure 2.33 provide another example of grouping, with projects grouped by Complete and Incomplete.

	ⓘ	Task Mode	Task Name	Duration	Start	Finish
			⊟ % Complete: 0%	5d	10/29/10	11/22/10
7		🖳	Task 5	3.75 days	10/29/10	11/3/10
8	ⅰ	🖳	Task 6	5 days	11/3/10	11/10/10
9	ⅰ	🖳	Task 7	5 days	11/8/10	11/15/10
10		🖳	Task 8	5 days	11/15/10	11/22/10
			⊟ % Complete: 1% - 99%	5d	10/22/10	10/28/10
6		🖳	Task 4	5 days	10/22/10	10/28/10
			⊟ % Complete: 100%	5d	10/4/10	10/21/10
2	✓	🖳	Task 1	4 days	10/4/10	10/7/10
3	✓	🖳	Task 2	5 days	10/8/10	10/14/10
4	✓	🖳	Task 3	5 days	10/15/10	10/21/10

Figure 2.33   *Projects are grouped by Complete and Incomplete in the Gantt Chart view.*

You can group data in a view in two ways. If the data you want to group is displayed in the view, click the arrow on the right side of the column header, click **Group By**, and then click the grouping option that meets your needs.

You can also group the data in a view using the ribbon by following these steps:

1. On the **View** tab of the ribbon, in the **Data** group, choose the criterion you want to use to group data from the **Group By** list.

2. If the criterion you want to group by is not listed, click **More Groups** if you think the grouping is already set up, or click **New Group By** to set up a new grouping.

3. To set up a new grouping, in the **Group Definition** dialog box, complete the following:

   - **Name**—Give the grouping a name.
   - **Show in Menu**—Select this check box to display the grouping in the **Group By** list.
   - **Group By**—Click the **Field Name** column in the **Group By** row, and then click the name of the first field you want to group by. Click the **Order** column in the **Group By** row to choose whether you want the data in the field you selected to be displayed in **Ascending** or **Descending** order.
   - **Then By**—Complete each **Then By** row, as needed, to create subgroups within each group. For example, if you chose to group by **Type**, in a resource view, you might find it helpful to create a subgroup within that group to sort by **Base Calendar**. This would show all work resources, for example, that use a night shift calendar together in a resource view.

Figure 2.34 shows an example of how to set up tasks to be grouped first by whether they're critical, and then by their percent complete.

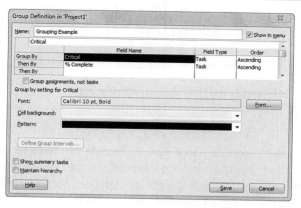

Figure 2.34 *The Group Definition dialog box with a grouping example*

4. Use the plus or minus signs next to the group rollups to expand or collapse each group.

5. Click **Clear Group** in the **Group By** list to remove the grouping from the view.

 SHOW ME   Media 2.5—Sort Data in a View

Access this video file through your registered Web Edition at my.safaribooksonline.com/9780132182461/media.

 LET ME TRY IT

Sorting Data in a View

By sorting data in a view, you choose the order in which you want data to appear. For example, you may want a list of names to be displayed in order from A to Z, or you may want a list of dates to be displayed from earliest to latest. Figure 2.35 shows the Gantt Chart view sorted by Duration.

		Task Mode	Task Name	Duration	Start	Finish
5			⊟ Phase 2	21.25 days	10/22/10	11/22/10
6			Task 4	5 days	10/22/10	10/28/10
8	⚡		Task 6	5 days	11/3/10	11/10/10
9	⚡		Task 7	5 days	11/8/10	11/15/10
10			Task 8	5 days	11/15/10	11/22/10
7			Task 5	3.75 days	10/29/10	11/3/10
1	✓		⊟ Phase 1	14 days	10/4/10	10/21/10
3	✓		Task 2	5 days	10/8/10	10/14/10
4	✓		Task 3	5 days	10/15/10	10/21/10
2	✓		Task 1	4 days	10/4/10	10/7/10

Figure 2.35   *The Gantt Chart view with data sorted by Duration*

There are two ways to sort data in a view. If the data you want to sort is displayed in the view, you can click the arrow on the right side of the column header and then choose the sort option from the list that appears. For example, if you click the arrow on the right side of the **Duration** column header, you can choose **Sort Smallest to Largest** or **Sort Largest to Smallest**.

You can also sort the data in a view using the ribbon by following these steps:

1. On the **View** tab of the ribbon, in the **Data** group, click **Sort**.

2. Choose a criterion you want to sort by, or, if none of the existing options meet your needs, click **Sort By** to create a custom sort order.

3. To create a custom sort order, on the **Sort** dialog box, choose the first field you want to use in the **Sort by** list, and then choose whether you want to sort in **Ascending** or **Descending** order. If you want to refine the sort order using additional fields, choose those fields from the **Then by** lists, and choose orders for those fields as well. Figure 2.36 shows an example of a sort order where tasks will first be sorted by Duration, then by Start.

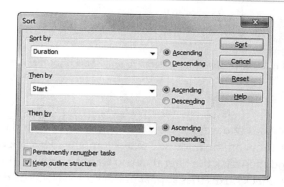

Figure 2.36 *An example of setting up a custom order*

4. Click **Sort** to sort the view using this custom sort order.

 SHOW ME   Media 2.6—Filter Data in a View
Access this video file through your registered Web Edition at
my.safaribooksonline.com/9780132182461/media.

 **LET ME TRY IT**

Filtering Data in a View

Filtering data can help by narrowing down the data displayed in a view. For example, let's say you're trying to find a resource with a particular skillset. If you've set Project 2010 up with a field for capturing resource skillsets, you can filter by that field in the **Resource Sheet** view to see only resources that meet your needs. Figure 2.37 shows this filter applied to the **Resource Sheet** view, looking only for Testers.

Resource Name	▼	Type	▼	Skillset	▼
Sonia		Work		Tester	
Vince		Work		Tester	
Jasper		Work		Tester	

Figure 2.37 *The Resource Sheet view filtered to only show resources with "Tester" in the Skillset column*

Project 2010 provides two ways to filter data in a view. To filter data that appears in a view, click the arrow on the right side of a column header, click **Filter** in the list that appears, and then click the filter that you want to apply to the column. You can also use the check boxes that appear in the list to select the data you want to appear. You can filter multiple columns in a view using this method.

You can also filter a view using the ribbon by following these steps:

1. On the **View** tab of the ribbon, in the **Data** group, choose a filtering option from the **Filter** list.

2. If the filter that you want to apply is not listed, click **More Filters** if you think the filter is already set up. Otherwise, click **New Filter**.

3. To set up a new filter, in the **Filter Definition** dialog box, complete the following:

   • **Name**—Give the filter a name.

   • **Show in menu**—Select this check box to display the filter in the **Filter** list.

   • **Filter**—Complete the first row of the grid to indicate what field you want to filter on and what you want to look for with that field. Choose the field name, test, and value(s) for the filter. For example, if you want to create a filter that looks for cost overages, you might choose **Actual Cost** in the

Field Name column, **is greater than** in the **Test** column, and **[Baseline Cost]** in the **Value(s)** column. You can include multiple rows in the filter to add conditions and use the **And/Or** column to indicate whether the filter should include all conditions or just select conditions.

Figure 2.38 shows an example of a filter definition that will show only Testers that have 100% of their time available to your project.

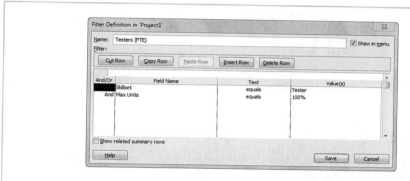

Figure 2.38   *An example of a filter definition*

4. Click **Apply** to apply the filter to the view, and then click **Save** to save the filter for future use.

5. Click **Clear Filter** in the **Filter** list to remove the filter from the view.

 SHOW ME   Media 2.7—Highlight Data in a View
Access this video file through your registered Web Edition at
my.safaribooksonline.com/9780132182461/media.

 LET ME TRY IT

Highlighting Data in a View

When you're working with a project, it can be helpful to have certain tasks, dates, or other information called out with a visual indicator for easy identification. Project 2010 enables you to set up data highlight filters based on conditions that you define. Figure 2.39 shows the Gantt Chart view, with tasks using a specific resource highlighted.

	ⓘ	Task Mode	Task Name	Duration	Start	Finish
1	✓		⊟ Phase 1	14 days	10/4/10	10/21/10
2	✓		Task 1	4 days	10/4/10	10/7/10
3	✓		Task 2	5 days	10/8/10	10/14/10
4	✓		Task 3	5 days	10/15/10	10/21/10
5			⊟ Phase 2	21.25 days	10/22/10	11/22/10
6			Task 4	5 days	10/22/10	10/28/10
7			Task 5	3.75 days	10/29/10	11/3/10
8	⫶		Task 6	5 days	11/3/10	11/10/10
9	⫶		Task 7	5 days	11/8/10	11/15/10
10			Task 8	5 days	11/15/10	11/22/10

Figure 2.39   *Tasks with the "Van #1" resource assigned are highlighted.*

Here are the steps to follow to highlight data in a view:

1. On the **View** tab of the ribbon, in the **Data** group, choose a highlight filter from the **Highlight** list.

2. If the highlight filter that you want to apply is not listed, click **More Highlight Filters** if you think the filter is already set up. Otherwise, click **New Highlight Filter**.

3. To set up a new highlight filter, in the **Filter Definition** dialog box, complete the following:

   • **Name**—Give the highlight filter a name.

   • **Show in menu**—Select this check box to display the filter in the **Highlight** list.

   • **Filter**—Complete the first row of the grid to indicate what field you want to filter on and what you want to look for with that field. Choose the field name, test, and value(s) for the filter. For example, if you want to create a filter that highlights tasks that you haven't baselined, you might choose **Baseline Start** in the **Field Name** column, **equals** in the **Test** column, and type **NA** in the **Value(s)** column. You can include multiple rows in the filter to add conditions, and use the **And/Or** column to indicate whether the filter should include all conditions or just select conditions.

   Figure 2.40 shows an example of how to set up a highlight filter for tasks that are critical, and that finished later than planned.

4. Click **Apply** to apply the highlight filter to the view, and then click **Save** to save the filter for future use.

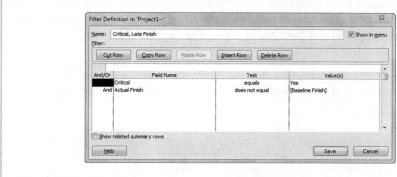

Figure 2.40   *An example of the settings for a highlight filter*

5. Click **Clear Highlight** in the **Highlight** list to remove the filter from the view.

SHOW ME   Media 2.8—Display Two Views at Once
Access this video file through your registered Web Edition at
my.safaribooksonline.com/9780132182461/media.

LET ME TRY IT

Displaying Two Views at Once

At times, it may be helpful to show more than one view in the Project window at the same time. The viewing area of the Project window can be split into two panes. The top pane can contain the Timeline view or another overall view of your project, such as the Gantt Chart view.

When the top pane displays the Timeline view, the bottom pane can display any other Project view. With the Timeline view in the top pane and the Gantt Chart view in the bottom pane, you can drag the highlighted box in the Timeline view horizontally to change the focus of the Gantt chart timeline.

To display the Timeline view, follow these steps:

1. On the **View** tab of the ribbon, in the **Split View** group, select the **Timeline** check box.

2. Click once in the **Timeline** view and then use the options on the **Format** tab to change the display options and data used in the **Timeline** view.

When the top pane displays another overall view of your project, the bottom pane is typically used to display one of the detail views, including the **Resource Form**, the **Resource Graph**, or the **Task Form** view, as shown in Figure 2.41.

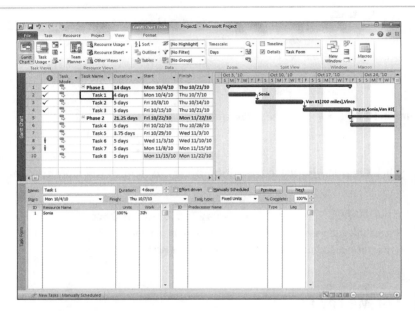

Figure 2.41 *Display the Gantt Chart view and the Task Form view at the same time to easily enter task details.*

With this configuration, clicking a task or resource in the top pane focuses the details displayed in the bottom pane. For example, if you have the **Gantt Chart** view displayed in the top pane, and the **Task Form** view displayed in the bottom pane, when you click a task in the **Gantt Chart** view, that task's details are displayed in the **Task Form** view.

To display a detail view in the bottom pane, follow these steps:

1. On the **View** tab of the ribbon, in the **Split View** group, select the **Details** check box.

2. Click the name of the detail view you want to display in the **Details** list.

3. To change the display options for either displayed view, click once in the pane that displays the view you want to modify and then click the **Format** tab.

This chapter covers how to start planning a project using Project 2010.

3

Starting a Project

The process of creating a plan in Project 2010 begins before work is done on any part of a project, before the schedule is set, before tasks are even identified. Creating a new project in Project 2010 means setting up the framework for the plan, and making some decisions about how the plan will be carried out, when people will be working on it, and what factors matter most while work is being done on the project.

 TELL ME MORE   Media 3.1—Top-Down Versus Bottom-Up
Project Planning
Access this audio recording through your registered Web Edition at
my.safaribooksonline.com/9780132182461/media.

Setting Up a Project

The first step to starting a project in Project 2010 is setting up the file and choosing where to save it.

 SHOW ME   Media 3.2—Create a New Project File
Access this video file through your registered Web Edition at
my.safaribooksonline.com/9780132182461/media.

 LET ME TRY IT

Creating a New Project

When you're ready to begin planning a project in Project 2010, start by creating a new file. You can create a new, blank plan; you can use a template; or you can create a new plan based on an existing project, Excel workbook, or SharePoint task list.

Some organizations may use Project Professional 2010 with Project Server for an end-to-end enterprise management solution. Projects are saved to Project Server, making them available to other project managers, portfolio managers, team members, or other users. If you are using Project Professional 2010 and want to save your new project to Project Server, be sure you are connected to Project Server before creating your new project. If you're not sure how to connect to Project Server, contact your organization's site administrator.

Follow these steps to create a new project:

1. Click the **File** tab and then click **New** on the left side of the Project window.

2. Choose how you want to create your new project, as shown in Figure 3.1.

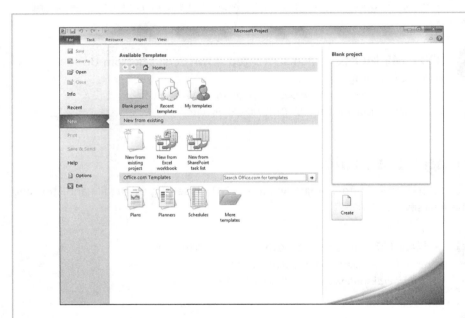

Figure 3.1 *Choose a method for creating a new project.*

- **Blank Project**—Click this option and then click **Create** on the right portion of the window to create a new project from scratch.
- **Recent Templates**—Click this option, click a template, and then click **Create** on the right portion of the screen to create a new project using a template that you have recently used.

- **My Templates**—Click this option, click a template, and then click **OK** to create a new project using a template that you have created or stored on your computer.

- **New from Existing Project**—Click this option, locate and click an existing project, and then click **Create New** to create a new project using an existing project as a starting point.

- **New from Excel Workbook**—Click this option, locate and click an Excel workbook, and then click **Open** to create a new project using data stored in the selected workbook. A wizard will walk you through the data-importing process.

- **New from SharePoint Task List**—Click this option, provide a URL for an existing SharePoint site, choose a task list from that site, and then click **OK** to create a new project using data from that list.

- **Office.com Templates**—Choose any of the options in this section or type a search query in the **Search Office.com for Templates** box to download and use a template from Office.com for your new project.

 LET ME TRY IT

Saving a Project

With your new project created, the next step is to decide where you want to save it. If you are using Project Professional 2010 and Project Server, you can choose to save the project to Project Server, making it possible to share your project with others in your organization using Project Web App. Project Web App is the Web interface for Project Server. It can be used for project planning, proposing new projects, capturing progress on existing projects, and business intelligence reporting.

To save your project on your computer or on a network share to which you have access, follow these steps:

1. Click the **File** tab and then click **Save** on the left side of the Project window.

2. Type a filename for the new project in the **File Name** box, locate where you want to save the project, and then click **Save**.

Project 2010 files cannot be opened using previous versions of Project. Instead, you can save your Project 2010 file to a format used by a previous version. Follow these steps:

1. Click the **File** tab and then click **Save As** on the left side of the Project window.

2. Type a filename in the **File Name** box, and then locate where you want to save the project,

3. In the **Save As Type** list, click **Microsoft Project 2007** or **Microsoft Project 2000 – 2003**, as shown in Figure 3.2.

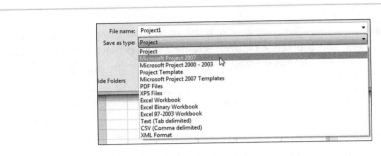

Figure 3.2   *Choose a previous version from the Save As Type list.*

4. Click **Save** to save the file using a previous version format.

Follow these steps to save your project to Project Server using Project Professional 2010:

1. Click the **File** tab and then click **Save** on the left side of the Project window.

2. Type a name for the new project in the **Name** box.

3. Click **Value** and select a value to complete any appropriate or required enterprise custom fields for the project. Required fields are marked with an asterisk (*).

4. Click **Save**.

With your project saved to Project Server, a couple of considerations need to be made if you want to share your project with others:

*   **Check your project in**—After saving your project to Project Server, you can begin planning, but the changes will not be available to others with the appropriate permissions to open the project until you check it in. To check your project in, click the **File** tab and then click **Close**. Checked-in projects can be checked out by people with the appropriate permissions.

*   **Publish your project**—People who are assigned to tasks in your project will not be able to view or enter project data using Project Web App until you have published the project. To publish the project, click the **File** tab and then click **Publish**.

Setting Project Properties and Options

You can set a lot of different options and defaults for your project—way too many to cover in a reasonable way when you're just getting started with your project. I do, however, point you to the ones that are the most important and the most commonly used at this point in your project.

 SHOW ME   Media 3.3—A Quick Look at Properties and Options

Access this video file through your registered Web Edition at
my.safaribooksonline.com/9780132182461/media.

 LET ME TRY IT

Setting Project Properties

First, look at setting project properties:

1. Click the **File** tab and then, with **Info** selected on the left side of the Project window, click **Project Information** on the right side of the window.

2. Click **Advanced Properties**, as shown in Figure 3.3.

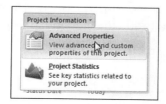

Figure 3.3   *Click Project Information, and then click Advanced Properties.*

3. On the **Summary** tab, provide whatever data is most appropriate in your organization. You can choose to include a **Title**, **Subject**, **Author**, **Manager**, **Company**, and other relevant metadata for your project, as shown in Figure 3.4.

Figure 3.4   *The Summary tab of the Properties dialog box contains metadata for your project.*

4. On the **Custom** tab, shown in Figure 3.5, you can include additional project properties by choosing a property **Name**, the data **Type** for the property, and the **Value** for the property. When all three of these fields are completed, click **Add** to add the property to your project.

5. Click **OK** to save your project's properties.

Setting Project Options

In addition to project properties, you can set several project options to control how different aspects of your project behave. At this point, it's probably best to use the default settings until you have a better idea of your project management needs. When you begin to identify things that aren't working the way you'd like, look at Chapter 10, "Understanding Project Options," for a detailed review of each option available on the Project Options dialog box.

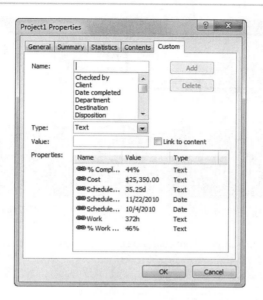

Figure 3.5   *Set custom metadata on the Custom tab of the Properties dialog box.*

Choosing a Project Start or Finish Date

A project can be scheduled from its start date or from its finish date, depending on whether you want to start it on a specific date or have it finished by a specific date.

To set a start or finish date for your project, follow these steps:

1. On the **Project** tab of the ribbon, in the **Properties** group, click **Project Information**.

2. Click the **Schedule from** box and then choose whether you want to schedule your project from the **Project Start Date** or the **Project Finish Date**.

3. Choose a project **Start Date** or **Finish Date**, as shown in Figure 3.6.

4. Click **OK** to save the date you selected.

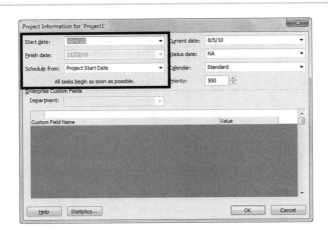

Figure 3.6 *Choose how you want your project to be scheduled and set the corresponding date.*

Setting Up Your Project's Calendars

Project 2010 uses calendars that identify working times to determine when resources in your organization are likely available to work on tasks in your project.

The four types of calendars are

- **Base calendars**—Project uses base calendars as a starting point for creating the other three types of calendars (project, task, and resource calendars). Use base calendars to enter holidays, typical working hours, and other organization-wide calendar items.

- **Project calendars**—Use a project calendar to set the default working times for all tasks in your project.

- **Task calendars**—Use task calendars to enter special days specific to individual tasks in your project. For example, if the task is to carry out an event that occurs over a weekend, you may want to change the working days for that task to include the weekend day as working time and replace the weekend day with a weekday as nonworking time.

- **Resource calendars**—Use resource calendars to track the schedules of individual resources. For example, if a resource has a flexible work arrangement and works four 10-hour days instead of five eight-hour days, you can set that resource's calendar to reflect that schedule, without changing the overall schedule for all other resources in the organization.

*The following sections talk about base and project calendars. For more information on task and resource calendars, **see** "Setting a task calendar" in Chapter 4, "Working with Tasks," and "Adjusting resource calendars" in Chapter 5, "Working with Resources."*

SHOW ME   Media 3.4—Setting Calendars and Working Times

Access this video file through your registered Web Edition at **my.safaribooksonline.com/9780132182461/media.**

LET ME TRY IT

Modifying an Existing Base Calendar

Project comes with three default base calendars already configured:

- **Standard**—8 A.M. to 5 P.M. weekdays, with a one-hour lunch break.

- **24 Hours**—8 A.M. to 4 P.M., 4 P.M. to 12 A.M., and 12 A.M. to 8 A.M., continuously, with no breaks.

- **Night Shift**—11 P.M. to 8 A.M. weekdays, with a one-hour break.

You can modify these base calendars to meet your organization's needs.

If you are using Project Professional 2010 with Project Server, the base calendars can be modified only by someone with appropriate permissions.

To choose which base calendar you want to modify, follow these steps:

1. On the **Project** tab, in the **Properties** group, click **Change Working Time.**

2. Click the **For Calendar** list and then click the base calendar you want to modify.

3. Review the working times displayed on the right portion of the **Change Working Time** dialog box. Click a day on the calendar to review its working times, as shown in Figure 3.7.

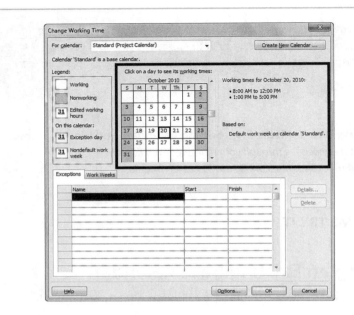

Figure 3.7 *Working times are displayed for the selected calendar day.*

 **LET ME TRY IT**

Changing a Working Day to a Nonworking Day

While on the **Change Working Time** dialog box, you can make several different kinds of changes to the selected base calendar.

Here's how to change a working day to a nonworking day (for example, to add a company holiday):

1. Click the day of the holiday in the calendar.

2. Type the name of the holiday in the **Name** column on the **Exceptions** tab and then press **Enter** to move to the next row and fill in the **Start** and **Finish** columns for the holiday.

3. If the holiday is observed on a regular basis, double-click the holiday, and then set a **Recurrence Pattern** and **Range of Recurrence** on the **Details** dialog box, as shown in Figure 3.8.

4. Click **OK** on the **Details** dialog box, and then click **OK** again on the **Change Working Time** dialog box to add the holiday to the selected base calendar.

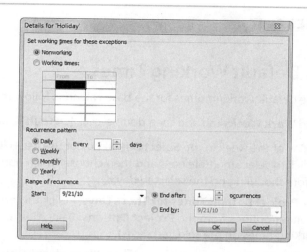

Figure 3.8 *Set details about calendar exceptions.*

 **LET ME TRY IT**

Changing a Nonworking Day to a Working Day

To change a nonworking day to a working day (for example, for an event occurring over a weekend), follow these steps:

1. Click the day of the event in the calendar.

2. Type the name of the event in the **Name** column on the **Exceptions** tab and then press **Enter** to move to the next row and fill in the **Start** and **Finish** columns for the event.

3. Double-click the event and then click **Working Times** on the **Details** dialog box.

4. Use the **From** and **To** columns to define the working hours for the event.

5. If the event is scheduled on a regular basis, you can set a **Recurrence Pattern** and **Range of Recurrence**.

6. Click **OK** on the **Details** dialog box, and then click **OK** again on the **Change Working Time** dialog box to add the event to the selected base calendar.

 **LET ME TRY IT**

Changing Default Working Times

To change the default working times for the base calendar, follow these steps:

1. Click the **Work Weeks** tab and then double-click **[Default]**.

2. Click a day of the week in the **Select Day(s)** box or use Ctrl+click or Shift+click to select multiple days and then choose which option you want to use for scheduling on the selected day(s):

   - **Use Project Default Times for These Days**—Click this option to use the calendar options from the **Project Options** dialog box to define the working times on the selected day(s).

   - **Set Days to Nonworking Time**—Click this to identify the selected day(s) as planned days off.

   - **Set Day(s) to These Specific Working Times**—Click this and use the **From** and **To** columns to identify the working times for the selected day(s), as shown in Figure 3.9.

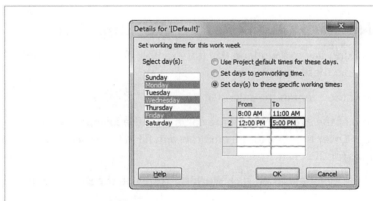

Figure 3.9 *Set different working times for specific days.*

3. Click **OK** to change the default working times for the selected base calendar.

LET ME TRY IT

Changing Working Times for a Specific Time Period

You may have specific weeks when the working times need to be different from the default working times. For example, if your organization has a week-long training session that limits the amount of project time to half-days for that week, you can include the schedule changes for that week in the base calendar.

Follow these steps to change the working times for a specific time period in the base calendar:

1. Click the **Work Weeks** tab and then type a name for the changed period of working time in the **Name** column.

2. Choose the start date for the changed period in the **Start** column and then choose the finish date in the **Finish** column.

3. Double-click the row you just created to bring up the **Details** dialog box.

4. Click a day of the week in the **Select day(s)** box, or use Ctrl+click or Shift+click to select multiple days, and then choose which option you want to use for scheduling on the selected day(s):

   - **Use Project default times for these days**—Click this to use the calendar options from the **Project Options** dialog box to define the working times on the selected day(s).

   - **Set days to nonworking time**—Click this to identify the selected day(s) as planned days off.

   - **Set day(s) to these specific working times**—Click this and use the **From** and **To** columns to identify the working times for the selected day(s).

5. Click **OK** to add the changed working times to the selected base calendar.

LET ME TRY IT

Creating a New Base Calendar

If none of the default base calendars meet your needs, you can create a new base calendar to use as a starting point for the project, task, and resource calendars.

If you are using Project Professional 2010 with Project Server, you can only create a new base calendar if you have the appropriate permissions.

Here's how to create a new base calendar:

1. On the **Project** tab, in the **Properties** group, click **Change Working Time**.

2. Click **Create New Calendar**.

3. Choose how you want to create the calendar:

   - **Create a New Base Calendar**—Click this option to create a new calendar from scratch. Working times will be set to the calendar options from the **Project Options** dialog box, by default.

   - **Make a Copy of [Existing Base] Calendar**—Click this option to use an existing base calendar as a starting point for your new base calendar. Use the drop-down list to choose which base calendar you want to copy.

4. Type a name for your new base calendar in the **Name** box, as shown in Figure 3.10.

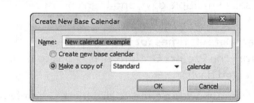

Figure 3.10 *Create a new blank calendar or base one off of an existing calendar.*

5. Click **OK** to create your new base calendar.

Use the steps in the previous section, "Modifying an Existing Base Calendar," to do the following:

- Change a working day to a nonworking day.

- Change a nonworking day to a working day.

- Change the default working times for the new base calendar.

- Change the working times for a specific time period in the new base calendar.

LET ME TRY IT

Setting Up Your Project's Calendar

When setting up your project's calendar, you need to decide which base calendar you want to use as a starting point. If most of your tasks need to be completed during normal working hours, choose the **Standard** base calendar. If most of your tasks need to be completed during off hours, the **Night Shift** base calendar may make more sense for your project. Or, if your project needs continuous coverage, choose the **24 Hours** base calendar.

If you are using Project Professional 2010 with Project Server, you can only modify the project calendar if you have the appropriate permissions.

If you need to change the working times in your project, consider modifying the task or resource calendars, as described in "Setting a task calendar" in Chapter 4 or "Adjusting resource calendars" in Chapter 5.

Remember that when you set the project calendar, you are simply choosing what the default working times will be for tasks and resources in your project. You can modify working times for individual tasks and resources to reflect exceptions to the default hours.

To set your project's calendar, follow these steps:

1. On the **Project** tab of the ribbon, in the **Properties** group, click **Project Information**.

2. Click **Calendar** and choose the base calendar that you want to use for your project, as shown in Figure 3.11.

3. Click **OK**.

4. On the **Project** tab, in the **Properties** group, click **Change Working Time**.

5. Ensure that the base calendar you selected in step 2 is displayed in the **For calendar** list.

6. Review the working times displayed on the right portion of the **Change Working Time** dialog box. Click a day on the calendar to review its working times.

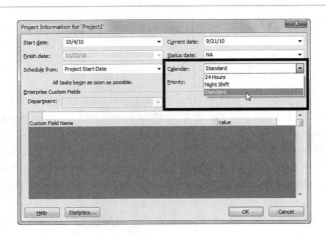

Figure 3.11   *Choose a base calendar to use for your project.*

7. Use the steps in the "Modifying an Existing Base Calendar" section to do the following:

    • Change a working day to a nonworking day.

    • Change a nonworking day to a working day.

    • Change the default working times for the project calendar.

    • Change the working times for a specific time period in the project calendar.

8. Click **OK** to save your changes.

How Does Project 2010 Schedule Tasks?

Talk about opening a can of worms! Although we could tackle this subject in a million ways, here's our best shot at summing up how tasks are scheduled in Project 2010. It's important to have a basic understanding of this before you head into the next chapter, where you'll start adding tasks to your project.

Scheduling Methods in Project 2010

Project 2010 offers two scheduling methods: automatic and manual. With manual scheduling, the project manager fully controls the task's start and finish dates. The Project scheduling engine does not come into play, and the dates the project manager sets for a task stay exactly as they're set, regardless of any other factors that may change in the project or with the resources assigned to the task. As you might imagine, there are plusses and minuses to this approach. The big plus is that there is no guessing game about what's impacting a manually scheduled task's dates. If you know a task needs to occur at a certain time, you may find manual scheduling easier to cope with than trying to manipulate other task dates and resource availabilities to get the right dates for the task in question. However, the downside to manual scheduling is that you don't get the project management assistance offered by the Project scheduling engine. This may make more sense after you have an understanding of automatic scheduling.

Look at automatic scheduling as having your own personal project management assistant sitting next to you to remind you of all the little things that are easy to overlook when you're planning your project. Need an example? Say that you know someone will be working full time on a task, and you assign that person to that task. Then, you change the duration for that task from 5 days to 10 days. With manual scheduling, the Work value for the task remains 40 hours. With automatic scheduling, when you increased the duration, the Work value also increased to 80 hours, to reflect the full time work across the new 10-day duration. Automatic scheduling helps you keep all of your bases covered, enabling you to craft an accurate and realistic schedule for your project.

What Factors Does the Project Scheduling Engine Consider?

When looking at when to schedule a task, the Project scheduling engine takes several things into account:

- **Project start and finish dates**—Depending on how you've decided to schedule your project, tasks will either be scheduled starting with the start date for the project or the finish date for the project. If a task date goes beyond the project start or finish date, a notification will appear.

- **Task factors**—The Project scheduling engine takes into account several task factors:

  - **Duration**—This is the amount of time each task is likely to take. Manually scheduled tasks also consider duration.

  - **Dependencies**—Some task dates may rely on when other tasks start or finish. In Project, these are called dependencies. Manually scheduled tasks also consider dependencies, to some extent.

  - **Lag/Lead Time**—This is the amount of time between the finish of one task and the start of the next, or the amount of time that one task needs to overlap another. Lag/lead time is captured when creating dependencies between tasks.

- **Constraints**—Some tasks may have to start or finish by a certain date. The Project scheduling engine will observe these date restrictions.

- **Task Types**—Tasks in your project fall under one of three different types, depending on whether time, amount of work, or number of resources is most important. When you have appropriately set the task type, the scheduling engine will protect that factor when adjusting the dates for that task.

- **Calendars**—The Project scheduling engine considers the working and nonworking time identified on the task calendars.

  *For more information about task factors, **see** Chapter 4.*

- **Resource Factors**—The Project scheduling engine takes into account several resource factors:

  - **Work**—This is the amount of time a resource likely will need to finish the task.

  - **Units**—This is a percentage that represents how much of a resource's overall time will be spent on the task.

  - **Calendars**—The Project scheduling engine considers the working and nonworking time identified on the resource calendars.

  *For more information about resource factors, **see** Chapter 5.*

The Task Inspector, included in Project 2010, helps you to find out what factors are affecting a task's start and finish dates. To display the Task Inspector, on the **Task** tab of the ribbon, in the **Tasks** group, click **Inspect** and then click **Inspect Task**.

Which Scheduling Method Should I Use?

Choosing whether to use manual scheduling or automatic scheduling really comes down to how much work you want to do to maintain your project's schedule, how well you understand how automatic scheduling works, and how much faith you have in the Project scheduling engine. Trust the Project scheduling engine (which, I assure you, was designed and developed by good, hard-working people who know what they're doing), use automatic scheduling for the bulk of your tasks, and use manual scheduling for one-off situations when your dates, resources, and amount of task work really are completely inflexible. Try your hardest not to resort to manual scheduling simply because you don't understand why Project is giving a task a certain start or finish date.

Here's an example that may help to convince you. First, follow these steps to see what you might run into if some of your tasks are manually scheduled:

1. On the **File** tab, click **New**, click **Blank Project**, and then click **Create**.

2. At the bottom of the Project window, click **New Tasks: Manually Scheduled**, and then click **Auto Scheduled – Task dates are calculated by Microsoft Project**.

3. In the **Task Name** column, create five tasks, labeled **Task 1** through **Task 5**.

4. In the **Task Mode** column for Task 3 and Task 4, choose **Manually Scheduled**.

5. Type **5d** in the **Duration** column for each task.

6. Type **Resource 1** in the **Resource Names** column for each task.

7. Select all five task rows by clicking the row header for Task 1, and the pressing **Shift** and clicking the row header for Task 5.

8. On the **Task** tab, in the **Schedule** group, click **Link Tasks**.

9. With your initial project plan created, type **10d** in the **Duration** column for Task 1, to represent an increase in the amount of work that needs to be done for that task.

Because of the dependencies between tasks, and the manual scheduling for Task 3 and Task 4, Resource 1 becomes overallocated on Task 2 and Task 3.

Now, let's look at what would happen if Task 3 and Task 4 were automatically scheduled, by continuing with these steps:

1. Press **Ctrl + Z** to undo the change to the duration for Task 1.

2. In the **Task Mode** column for Task 3 and Task 4, choose **Auto Scheduled**.

3. Type **10d** in the **Duration** column for Task 1.

With automatic scheduling, if a task's duration is extended, the predecessor tasks that are linked to the changed task are pushed out appropriately, with no unnecessary overallocations.

On a small project like the one used in this example, issues like the overallocations resulting from manually scheduled tasks are relatively easy to handle. There weren't very many tasks, there was only one resource involved, and manually rescheduling the involved tasks wouldn't have been too difficult. However, imagine if you were dealing with a large, complex project, with 300+ tasks and 100+ resources. Reviewing your project for issues resulting from manual scheduling may be time-consuming and unnecessary.

That said, there are times when manual scheduling is the right choice for tasks in your project. Here are a couple of examples:

- **Dates not defined**—When you are in the early planning stages of a project, you may not know what dates you're dealing with. Using manual scheduling, you can leave dates blank, or set to TBD, to include the task in the list, but leave it off of the Gantt chart.

- **Top-down scheduling**—In some cases, you may want to plan your project by providing high-level project start and finish dates, and then breaking those dates down into tasks. To do this, your project needs to use manual scheduling. With automatic scheduling, the dates for the tasks roll up and define the dates for the project. This is called bottom-up scheduling. With manual scheduling, you can plan the project in the other direction, starting with the project dates. This is called top-down scheduling.

At any point during a project, you can change a task from manual scheduling to automatic scheduling, or vice versa, using the Task Mode column. So, for example, you can do your initial project planning using top-down scheduling in manually scheduled mode, and then, once your schedule is set, switch to automatic scheduling to help monitor and maintain your initial schedule.

This chapter walks you through adding tasks to your project in Project 2010.

4

Working with Tasks

After you have created and saved your initial project plan, the next step is to add tasks to your project. It's important to understand the different types of tasks that Project 2010 offers. With a basic understanding of task types, you can add tasks to your project and then set up dependencies between the tasks. Project 2010 also provides a framework for adding work breakdown structure codes to your tasks, if your organization uses them.

Understanding Task Types

Each task in your project can be one of three different types:

- Fixed units

- Fixed work

- Fixed duration

These task types are used to determine which element of a task is most important for scheduling, so that Project knows what it should maintain as it sets your project's schedule. Project calculates the schedule using the following formula: **Duration = Work / Units**.

Table 4.1 shows what changes Project makes, based on task types, for a task that is set to automatic scheduling.

Table 4.1 Task Types

Task Type	Adjust Units	Adjust Work	Adjust Duration
Fixed units	Duration is adjusted.	Duration is adjusted.	Work is adjusted.
Fixed work	Duration is adjusted.	Duration is adjusted.	Units are adjusted.
Fixed duration	Work is adjusted.	Units are adjusted.	Work is adjusted.

Fixed Units

Fixed units is the task type to pick if the level of effort on your project is important to you. For example, let's say you assign a resource to a task, and you know you can only use that resource for that task half time. You assign the resource at 50% (units). After your initial planning, you find out that you need to make the task longer, or you discover that the task may take more work than you thought. You don't want Project to change the units, so you choose the fixed units task type. This leaves the resource assigned at 50%, and Project recalculates the work or duration, based on what factor you changed.

Looking at this from a formula perspective, say the original duration of the task is 5 days, the work is initially set to 20 hours, and the units is set to 50%. The formula would look like this: 5d = 20h / 50%. If the task is fixed units, you can't change the 50%.

- **Changed duration**—If the duration is increased to 10 days, Project will adjust the 20 hours of work to maintain a balanced equation: 10d = 40h / 50%. Because the task is set to fixed units, the resource will always work at 50%. So if you increase the duration, the resource will work more hours. Project will increase the work to 40 hours.

- **Changed work**—If the work is increased to 40 hours, Project will adjust the 5 days of duration, because the resource is only able to work at 50%, or 20 hours per week. It will take the resource 10 days to get 40 hours of work done, working 20 hours per week. This adjustment maintains a balanced equation: 10d = 40h / 50%.

Fixed Work

If a task is set to **fixed work**, Project will maintain the amount of work scheduled for the task. Look again at the previous example: 5d = 20h / 50%.

- **Changed units**—If you need to keep the task set to 20 hours of work, and you find out that your resource is only available at 25% instead of 50%, Project will adjust the duration to 10 days because it will take the resource longer to get the work done if he or she is working fewer hours each week. This maintains a balanced equation: 10d = 20h / 25%.

- **Changed duration**—If you find out that you have 10 days to get the task done, instead of 5, Project will adjust the units to 25%, because it will take less of the resource's time each week to get the work done. This maintains a balanced equation: 10d = 20h / 25%.

Fixed Duration

If a task is set to fixed duration, Project will maintain the length of time you've set aside to complete the task. Again, return to the example: 5d = 20h / 50%.

- **Changed work**—If the amount of work increases to 40 hours, with the duration fixed at 5 days, Project will adjust the resource units. Instead of 50%, the task now requires 100% to get 40 hours of work done in 5 days. The balanced equation is: 5d = 40h / 100%. You can get to 100% by increasing the amount of time the existing resource works in a week, or by assigning additional resources to the task.

- **Changed units**—If you find out that the resource assigned to the task is now available at 100% of his or her time, Project will adjust the amount of work for the task, to maintain the 5 days of duration: 5d = 40h / 100%. Because the resource is assigned at 100%, he or she can fit in 40 hours of work in 5 days, instead of 20 hours.

 SHOW ME   Media 4.1—Learn More About Task Types
Access this video file through your registered Web Edition at
my.safaribooksonline.com/9780132182461/media.

Adding Tasks to Your Project

When adding tasks to your project in Project 2010, you can choose to fill out a lot of detail about your tasks upfront, or you can enter some basic scheduling information at first and then fill in more details later.

 SHOW ME   Media 4.2—Working with Tasks
Access this video file through your registered Web Edition at
my.safaribooksonline.com/9780132182461/media.

 LET ME TRY IT

Adding a New Task

To add a new task to your project, follow these steps:

1. In the **Gantt Chart** view, type a name for the new task in the first empty row of the **Task Name** column.

To insert a new task between two existing tasks, right-click a task row and click **Insert Task** to add a new row above.

2. Click the **Task Mode** column and then choose whether you want the task to be **Manually Scheduled** or **Auto Scheduled**. Project uses one of these methods as a default. You only need to choose a method if you don't want to use what is set as the default.

☞ *Not sure whether you want Manually Scheduled or Auto Scheduled? Review "How Does Project 2010 Schedule Tasks?" in Chapter 3, "Starting a Project," for more information on scheduling in Project 2010 or view Show Me Media 4.3. If you choose Manually Scheduled, be sure to listen to Tell Me More Media 4.4 for some best practices.*

3. Type the number of days over which you want the task work completed in the **Duration** column. You also can use minutes (m), hours (h), weeks (w), or months (mo) if one of these would be more appropriate for your project.

4. Set the task's **Start** and **Finish** dates:
   - If you selected **Auto Scheduled** in step 2, the **Start** and **Finish** columns will be populated automatically with the appropriate dates, based on the project scheduling options you chose when you created the project (see Chapter 3). Do not manually set a start or finish date if you are using automatic scheduling.
   - If you selected **Manually Scheduled** in step 2, choose a **Start** date, and Project will fill in a **Finish** date. Alternatively, choose a **Finish** date, and Project will fill in a **Start** date. Project calculates the **Start** or **Finish** date using the information you entered in the **Duration** column.

5. To set additional task details, go to the **Task** tab of the ribbon. In the **Properties** group, click **Details** to display the **Task Details Form** view split with the **Gantt Chart** view, as shown in Figure 4.1.

6. Use the **Task Details Form** view to set the following:
   - **Task type**—Choose whether the task is **Fixed Duration**, **Fixed Units**, or **Fixed Work**.
   - **Constraint**—By default, this field is set to **As Soon As Possible**, meaning that the task could happen at any appropriate time in the project. You also can choose **As Late As Possible**, if that makes more sense for your project. However, you may have some tasks that need to happen in coordination with a specific date. You can choose from the following constraints: **Finish No Earlier Than**, **Finish No Later Than**, **Must Finish**

On, Must Start On, Start No Earlier Than, and **Start No Later Than**. If you choose one of these constraints, be sure to choose an associated date using the **Date** box within the **Constraint** box.

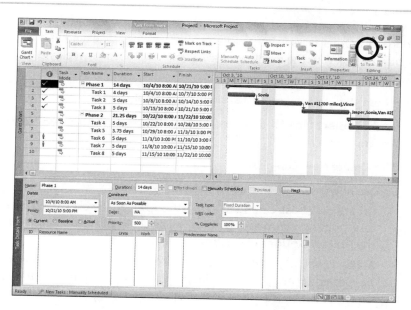

Figure 4.1   *Click Details on the Task tab to display the Task Details Form view, split with the Gantt Chart view.*

When choosing a constraint for a task, keep in mind that what you choose can impact Project's ability to do things like enforce links to other tasks and properly distribute resource work on the task.

7. Click **OK** to save your task settings.

SHOW ME   Media 4.3—Automatic Versus Manual Scheduling
Access this video file through your registered Web Edition at
my.safaribooksonline.com/9780132182461/media.

TELL ME MORE   Media 4.4—Best Practices for Working with Manually Scheduled Tasks
Access this audio file through your registered Web Edition at
my.safaribooksonline.com/9780132182461/media.

Setting a Task Calendar

Sometimes, a task in your project may need to use a different schedule from the rest of your project. For example, let's say a specific task needs to happen over a weekend. The overall project calendar has the weekends set as nonworking days. You can set a separate calendar for that task, so that the weekend days are set as working days. Other tasks in your project will still see the weekend as nonworking days, but the task with the modified task calendar will see the weekend as working days.

Follow these steps to set a separate calendar for a task:

1. On the **Project** tab of the ribbon, in the **Properties** group, click **Change Working Time**.

2. Click **Create New Calendar**.

3. Choose how you want to create the task's calendar:

    • **Create new base calendar**—Click this to create a new calendar for your task, from scratch. Working times will be set to the calendar options from the **Project Options** dialog box, by default.

    • **Make a copy of [existing base] calendar**—Click this to use an existing base calendar as a starting point for your task's calendar. Use the drop-down list to choose which base calendar you want to copy.

4. Type a name for your task's calendar in the **Name** box. You may want to use a name that helps to identify this as a calendar that is intended for use on a specific task. This will help to differentiate it from the base calendars for your project.

5. Click **OK** to create your task's calendar.

6. Similar to creating a base calendar, set the working days, nonworking days, default working times, and working times for specific time periods in your task's calendar.

⊙ *For more information on these procedures,* **see** *"Setting Up Your Project's Calendars" in Chapter 3.*

7. With your task's calendar set up and saved, double-click the task row in the **Gantt Chart** view.

8. Click the **Advanced** tab and then choose the calendar you just created from the **Calendar** list.

9. Click **OK** to save the calendar setting.

Indenting and Outdenting Tasks

After you have a list of tasks added to your project, you may find that you want to add some organizational structure to your tasks. You can indent and outdent tasks to add hierarchy to your project. Tasks that have other tasks indented below them are called *summary tasks*. Tasks that are indented below another task are called *subtasks*. Summary tasks roll up data from their subtasks. For example, if a summary task has two subtasks, the summary task will take the earliest start date and the latest finish date from those subtasks, as shown in Figure 4.2.

Phase 1	**15 days**	**11/1/10**	**11/19/10**
Task A	5 days	11/1/10	11/5/10
Task B	5 days	11/8/10	11/12/10
Task C	5 days	11/15/10	11/19/10

Figure 4.2 *Subtasks roll up data to the summary task level.*

To indent or outdent a task, click the task in the **Gantt Chart** view to select it. Then, on the **Task** tab of the ribbon, in the **Schedule** group, click **Indent** or **Outdent**, as shown in Figure 4.3.

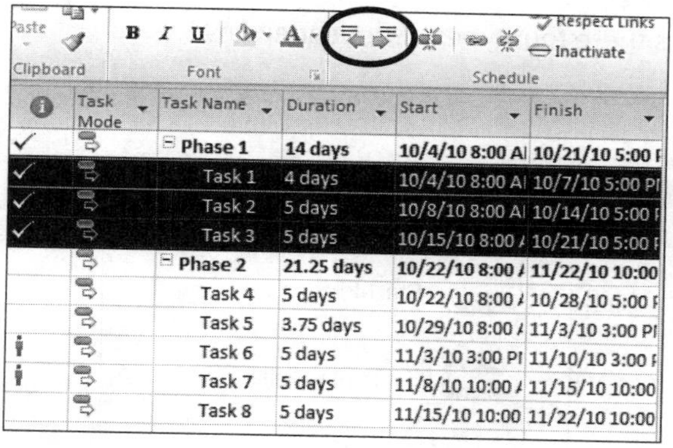

Task Mode	Task Name	Duration	Start	Finish
	Phase 1	**14 days**	**10/4/10 8:00 A**	**10/21/10 5:00**
	Task 1	4 days	10/4/10 8:00 A	10/7/10 5:00 P
	Task 2	5 days	10/8/10 8:00 A	10/14/10 5:00
	Task 3	5 days	10/15/10 8:00	10/21/10 5:00
	Phase 2	**21.25 days**	**10/22/10 8:00**	**11/22/10 10:00**
	Task 4	5 days	10/22/10 8:00	10/28/10 5:00
	Task 5	3.75 days	10/29/10 8:00	11/3/10 3:00 P
	Task 6	5 days	11/3/10 3:00 P	11/10/10 3:00
	Task 7	5 days	11/8/10 10:00	11/15/10 10:00
	Task 8	5 days	11/15/10 10:00	11/22/10 10:00

Figure 4.3 *Use the Indent and Outdent buttons to create hierarchy in your tasks.*

You can also choose to display the project summary task, which will roll all tasks and summary tasks up to the very top level of the project. To display the project summary task, click the **File** tab on the ribbon, click **Options**, and then click **Advanced**. Under **Display options for this project**, select the **Show project summary task** check box and then click **OK**.

Setting Up Task Dependencies

Some tasks in your project may have certain relationships with other tasks in your project. For example, you may have a task that can't begin until another task has ended. These relationships are called *dependencies*. Project offers four different types of dependencies for your project's tasks:

- **Finish-to-Start (FS)**—A finish-to-start dependency is one in which a second task cannot begin until the first task has ended.

- **Start-to-Start (SS)**—A start-to-start dependency is one in which a second task cannot begin until the first task has begun.

- **Finish-to-Finish (FF)**—A finish-to-finish dependency is one in which a second task cannot finish until the first task has finished.

- **Start-to-Finish (SF)**—A start-to-finish dependency is one in which a second task cannot finish until the first task has begun.

Figure 4.4 shows these four types of dependencies.

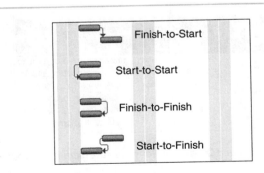

Figure 4.4 *Project provides four types of dependencies.*

Let's walk through an example that uses all four of these types of dependencies. In this example, you are planning to remodel the kitchen and dining area in a home. You use Project to track each of the tasks involved in this process.

Here are the tasks you want to track for the remodel:

- **Rewire kitchen**—This involves moving outlets, wiring through cabinets for a built-in microwave, and adding an outlet on a kitchen island.

- **Install new cabinets**—This involves installing new wall cabinets, and cabinets to support a new countertop.

- **Paint**—This involves painting both the kitchen and dining areas.

- **Install counters**—This involves placing a new countertop on top of the new cabinetry.

- **Install new floors**—This involves placing new flooring in both the kitchen and dining areas.

- **Install new appliances**—This involves installing several new kitchen appliances.

Each task has some sort of dependency on another task. The "Rewire kitchen" task can't be finished until the "Install new cabinets" task has started, because some of the wiring needs to be done through the new cabinetry (wiring for a built-in microwave, and an outlet on the island). This is a start-to-finish dependency in Project.

The "Paint" task has a start-to-start dependency on the "Rewire kitchen" task. That is, the painting can't start until the electrician has started the process of rewiring. The electrician needs to have moved openings for outlets and light fixtures, as necessary, before the painters can come in and begin painting the kitchen and dining areas. The electrician doesn't need to be done with all of his work for the remodel before the painters can start, just the portion of work that impacts the painters.

The "Install counters" task can't start until the "Paint" task has finished. By setting up this finish-to-start dependency, you avoid getting drips of paint all over the shiny new countertops. This type of dependency is most commonly used in project plans.

The "Install new floors" task can't finish until the "Paint" task has finished. The painters begin by painting the ceiling in both the kitchen and dining areas, then move on to painting the kitchen. After the kitchen is painted, the flooring installers begin their work in the kitchen, while the painters finish painting the dining room. The flooring team can't finish its work until the painters have finished painting the dining room. At that time, the flooring team can finish its work by flooring the dining room. In Project, this is represented as a finish-to-finish task.

Finally, the "Install new appliances" task can't start until the "Install new floors" task has finished. This is another finish-to-start dependency.

Project represents these task dependencies on the Gantt chart using arrows between the tasks. Figure 4.5 shows how our example might look if we entered it into Project and set up the dependencies.

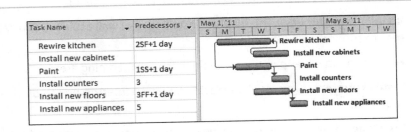

Figure 4.5   *Example of dependencies within a project*

 **LET ME TRY IT**

Adding Dependencies Between Tasks

In Project, dependencies between tasks are recorded in the row for the second task in the dependency. For example, if you are creating a dependency in which Task B can't start until Task A has finished (a finish-to-start dependency), you would record the dependency in the row for Task B. When you record the dependency, you indicate the task's *predecessor*.

To quickly set start-to-finish dependencies between tasks in your project, select the rows for the tasks you want to link, and then, on the **Task** tab, in the **Schedule** group, click **Link Tasks**.

If you want to set up other types of dependencies, create gaps between tasks, or overlap tasks, you can set up dependencies using the **Predecessors** column.

To set up a dependency between two tasks using the **Predecessors** column, follow these steps:

1.   In the **Gantt Chart** view, be sure the **Predecessors** column is displayed.

If the **Predecessors** column is not displayed, scroll all the way to the right of the table portion of the **Gantt Chart** view and then click **Add New Column**. Click **Predecessors** in the list that appears, to add the column to the view. You can click and drag the column header to move the column to another location in the table portion of the view.

2. In the row for the second task in the dependency you're creating, type the ID number (located in the row header) for the first task in the dependency in the **Predecessors** column. Also, indicate the dependency type.

    For example, if you are creating a dependency between Task A (ID number 1) and Task B (ID number 2), you would type the following for each dependency type:

    -   **Finish-to-start**—To indicate that Task B can't start until Task A finishes, type **1** in the **Predecessors** column for Task B, as shown in Figure 4.6. Project assumes a finish-to-start dependency, by default, so you don't need to include a dependency type abbreviation.

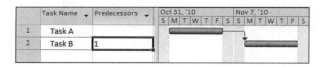

Figure 4.6   *In this example, Task B has a finish-to-start dependency on Task A.*

    -   **Start-to-start**—To indicate that Task B can start only after Task A has started, type **1SS** in the **Predecessors** column for Task B.
    -   **Finish-to-finish**—To indicate that Task B can finish only after Task A has finished, type **1FF** in the **Predecessors** column for Task B.
    -   **Start-to-finish**—To indicate that Task B can finish only after Task A has started, type **1SF** in the **Predecessors** column for Task B.

3. If one of your tasks needs to overlap another (known as "lead time"), or needs to fall behind another (known as "lag time") by a certain amount, type this in the **Predecessors** column, as well:

    -   **Overlap two tasks**—To overlap two tasks, type a negative duration, or percentage, after the task ID number and dependency type in the **Predecessors** column, as shown in Figure 4.7. For example, if you want Task B to start one day before Task A is scheduled to start, type **1SS-1d** in the **Predecessors** column for Task B.

Figure 4.7   *Insert lead time in the Predecessors column.*

- **Insert a delay between two tasks**—If the second task needs a delay after the start or finish of the first task, type a positive duration, or percentage, after the task ID number and dependency type in the **Predecessors** column, as shown in Figure 4.8. For example, if you want Task B to start when Task A is 50% through its scheduled duration, type **1SS+50%** in the **Predecessors** column for Task B.

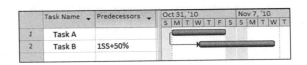

Figure 4.8   *Insert lag time in the Predecessors column.*

Creating a Work Breakdown Structure (WBS)

Some organizations require the use of a work breakdown structure to align project tasks with accounting systems, business strategies, and so on. It is a method of making sure that all work is accounted for, and decomposed into small enough packages for tracking and management. In Project, a work breakdown structure (WBS) is represented as an elaborate outline, providing each task with a WBS code that identifies where it falls within your project plan.

For example, let's say you have a project with the task structure shown in Table 4.2.

Table 4.2   Example Task Structure

Task Name		
Design Phase		
Identify requirements		
Conduct survey		
Prioritize results		
Write specification document		
Develop Phase		
Code product		
Write code		
Test code		

In a WBS code, each indent level in your task structure is given a set of letters, numbers, or characters that you define. For example, the phases in the example may be given a set of characters; the tasks may be given a number; and the subtasks may be given a lowercase letter. In Project, you can also assign a prefix for the code, to indicate the task's project. If you use the combination of characters, numbers, and letters just described, with a prefix of "EX_" to indicate that this is an example project, the WBS codes might be assigned as shown in Table 4.3.

Table 4.3   WBS Codes

Task Name	WBS Code	
Design Phase	EX_Design	
Identify requirements	EX_Design_1	
Conduct survey	EX_Design_1.a	
Prioritize results	EX_Design_1.b	
Write specification document	EX_Design_2	
Develop Phase	EX_Develop	
Code product	EX_Develop_1	
Write code	EX_Develop_1.a	
Test code	EX_Develop_1.b	

Note how the tasks and the WBS codes are starting to look like an outline. Project also includes an automatic outline scheme that simply uses increasing numbers, separated by periods, to indicate where a task falls within a project. Table 4.4 shows the example tasks, WBS codes, and their corresponding Project outline numbers.

Table 4.4   Outline Numbers

Task Name	WBS Code	Outline Number
Design Phase	EX_Design	1
Identify requirements	EX_Design_1	1.1
Conduct survey	EX_Design_1.a	1.1.1
Prioritize results	EX_Design_1.b	1.1.2
Write specification document	EX_Design_2	1.2
Develop Phase	EX_Develop	2
Code product	EX_Develop_1	2.1
Write code	EX_Develop_1.a	2.1.1
Test code	EX_Develop_1.b	2.1.2

To display outline numbers for your project, with the **Gantt Chart** view displayed, click the **Format** tab on the ribbon and then select the **Outline Number** check box in the **Show/Hide** group. The outline numbers appear to the left of each task's name.

Confused about when to use which? This depends on your organization. If you're just trying to identify where a task falls in your project, outline numbers may be enough. However, if you're using the numbers to sync with another system, or to communicate with others about your project, WBS codes provide a richer, more descriptive way of outlining your project's tasks.

 **LET ME TRY IT**

Setting Your Project's WBS Code Structure

You can set your project's WBS code structure at the beginning, before you have tasks added, if you know enough about how many levels of tasks you might use and what information the code needs to capture. You may, however, have an easier time building out your WBS code structure after you know what your project's tasks really look like.

Follow these steps to set up a WBS code structure for your project:

1. On the **Project** tab of the ribbon, in the **Properties** group, click **WBS** and then click **Define Code**.

2. If you want to use a prefix to identify which project the tasks belong to, type a prefix in the **Project Code Prefix** box, as shown in Figure 4.9.

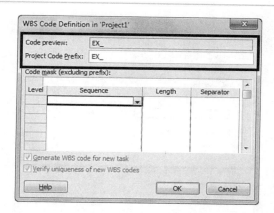

Figure 4.9   *Use the Project Code Prefix box to include text before the ordered portion of the code.*

As you build out your WBS code structure, the **Code preview** box shows an example of what your code will look like for a task at the lowest level in your project.

3. Use the columns and rows in the **Code mask** table to build out your WBS code structure. Each row represents an indent level for tasks in your project. Figure 4.10 shows a defined code mask.

    *   **Sequence**—Choose whether you want to use **Numbers, Uppercase Letters, Lowercase Letters**, or **Characters**.

If you choose to use **Characters**, the **Code preview** box shows an asterisk (*) as a placeholder for the characters, and you can type the characters in the WBS field for your project after you have your code structure set up.

- **Length**—Choose the number of characters you want to use for this part of your WBS code. If you choose one character and the number of tasks at this level goes beyond nine, a WBS code will not be assigned, and you'll receive an error message. Also, if you choose two or more characters, single-digit numbers will begin with a zero (01, 02, 03, and so on). If you want to avoid both of these circumstances, leave it set to **Any**.

- **Separator**—Choose a character to separate this part of your WBS code from the next part. You can choose one of the built-in separators (period, hyphen, plus sign, or slash), or type one of your own.

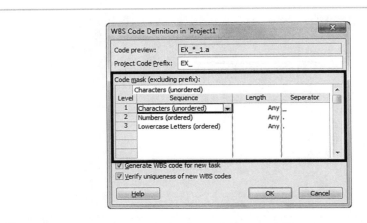

Figure 4.10   *Use the Code mask table to define your WBS code.*

4. Select the **Generate WBS code for new task** check box if you want to automatically create a WBS code for each task you add to your project.

5. Select the **Verify uniqueness of new WBS codes** check box if you want each WBS code to be unique. This can be helpful if you have used the **Characters** option in the **Sequence** column.

6. Click **OK** to save your WBS code structure.

After you have your WBS code structure set up, the next step is to display the WBS code in the **Gantt Chart** view, so you can see the fruits of your labor.

To display the WBS column, follow these steps:

1. With the **Gantt Chart** view displayed, right-click the column that you want to appear to the right of the **WBS** column.

2. Click **Insert Column** and then scroll down and click **WBS** from the menu that appears. Figure 4.11 shows the **Gantt Chart** view with the WBS code displayed.

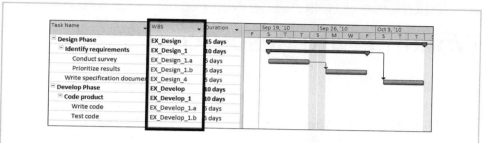

Figure 4.11   *The WBS column displays the WBS code for each task.*

5

Working with Resources

In Project, the people, things, and money you need to get the tasks in your project done are called *resources*. By adding resources to your project, you make them available to assign to tasks within your project. Resources can have calendars that are unique to them and can be assigned specific cost information.

> For a brief overview of resources, see "Resource" in Chapter 1, "Introduction to Managing Projects with Microsoft Project 2010."

Understanding Resource Types and Other Factors

Project supports three different types of resources:

- *Work resources* are the people and equipment that will do the work to complete tasks in your project. For example, a developer for your product is a work resource, and the server he uses to check code is also a work resource.

- *Material resources* are the things that the work resources need to complete tasks in your project. For example, if one of the work resources for your project is a plotter, you may also want to include material resources for paper and toner. Or, if you're planning a construction project, you may want to include cement, rebar, lumber, and other supplies for your project as material resources.

- *Cost resources* are the fees associated with getting tasks in your project done, which aren't associated with the amount of work put into a project or how long the project lasts. For example, if a task in your project requires a business trip, you would include the airfare and hotel charges as cost resources.

Cost resources are different from the costs incurred by work resources doing work on your project, or the costs incurred as you use material resources (supplies) to get work done. For more information on costs in your project, see Chapter 6, "Accounting for Project Costs."

TELL ME MORE   Media 5.1—Making Sense of Cost Resources
Access this audio recording through your registered Web Edition at
my.safaribooksonline.com/9780132182461/media.

In addition to these three types of resources, keep a couple other considerations in mind when planning your project:

- **Will other projects use the same resources as my project?** If the resources you'll be using in your project can also be used in other projects in your organization, and if you are running Project Professional 2010 with Project Server, you can choose to make resources in your project enterprise resources or assign enterprise resources to your project. An *enterprise resource* is a resource that is included in a list of all resources in your organization (the enterprise resource pool). By assigning resources from the enterprise resource pool, you are able to account for work that your resources are doing on other projects, not just your own. This helps track resource availability and enables you to more accurately plan your project within the broader scope of your organization.

- **Do I know exactly who/what will be working on my project?** If you know you'll need a specific kind of resource on your project, such as a developer or a roofer, but you're not sure exactly who or what will be doing the work (that is, you don't know which person or which server), you can use *generic resources* to plan your project. By assigning generic resources, you can identify just how many people or things your project will need, and then you can substitute them later for the specific people, equipment, or other resources that will be doing the work you have laid out in your project plan.

SHOW ME   Media 5.2—Adding a Resource
Access this video file through your registered Web Edition at
my.safaribooksonline.com/9780132182461/media.

Adding Resources to Your Project

The process for adding a resource to your project is different, depending on whether you're adding a resource used only in your project (a local resource) or an enterprise resource available for assignment throughout your organization (Project Professional only).

 LET ME TRY IT

To add a local resource to your project, follow these steps:

1. On the **View** tab, in the **Resource Views** group, click **Resource Sheet**.

2. Type the name of your work, material, or cost resource in the **Resource Name** column. If you are adding a generic resource, type a generic label for the resource, such as **Roofer**, **Web Server**, or **Designer**.

3. Choose whether the resource is a work, material, or cost resource using the list in the **Type** column.

4. If you chose **Material** in the **Type** column, type the unit label for the material resource in the **Material Label** column. For example, if you are adding fabric as a material resource, you might choose to type **yards** in the **Material Label** column.

5. If you want the resource to be part of a larger group of resources, such as employees in the same role or in the same department, type the name of the group in the **Group** column.

6. Type the maximum amount of the resource's time that can be spent on the project, as a decimal or percentage of the resource's time, in the **Max Units** column. For example, if a resource is working half-time on your project and half-time on other projects, type **50%** or **.5** in the **Max Units** column for that resource.

If you are adding a generic resource, you can use the **Max Units** column to identify how many of that generic resource you have available for your project. For example, if you have enough work for three full-time developers working on tasks in your project, you can enter **300%** in the **Max Units** column for the **Developer** generic resource.

7. If appropriate, type the cost information for the resource in the following fields:

   - **Std Rate**—Type the standard cost rate for the resource. That is, how much the resource is paid for specific time units, such as an hourly, daily, or yearly rate.

   - **Ovt Rate**—Type the overtime cost rate for the resource. That is, how much the resource is paid for overtime work in specific time units, such as per minute, per hour, or per day.

   - **Cost/Use**—Type a per-use cost for the resource, if applicable. For example, several tasks in your project will use an industrial printer. Each time you use the printer, there is an initial cost-per-use fee of $250 on top of the standard daily rate.

   - **Accrue at**—Choose when the costs will be accrued for the resource. By default, this is set to **Prorated**, meaning that the costs for this resource will be accrued as work is scheduled and actual work is reported on a task. If you choose **Start**, costs for the entire task will be accrued at the beginning of a resource's assignment, based on the scheduled work for the task. If you choose **End**, costs for the resource's task assignment will not be accrued until the remaining work for the task is set to 0.

8. If you are adding a generic resource, on the **Resource** tab, in the **Properties** group, click **Information**.

9. Select the **Generic** check box and click **OK**.

 LET ME TRY IT

Here's how to add an enterprise resource to your project, using Project Professional 2010:

1. On the **Resource** tab, in the **Insert** group, click **Add Resources**, and then click **Build Team from Enterprise**.

2. Use the **Existing filters** box to filter the list of enterprise resources.

3. Select the **Available to work** check box to narrow the list of resources to only those that are available to work a certain number of hours during a specific time range.

4. To find generic resources, click + to expand **Customize filters** and then define a filter:

   - **Field Name**—Generic
   - **Test**—Equals
   - **Values**—Yes

5. Click **Apply Filter** to display only generic resources.

6. After you decide which enterprise resources you want to add to your project, press Ctrl and click each resource in the **Enterprise Resource** column and then click **Add**.

7. Click **OK** to add the selected resources to your project.

Adjusting Resource Calendars

An individual resource within your project may use a different calendar from the rest of the organization. For example, one of your project's resources might be out on vacation for two weeks in the middle of July, or a specific piece of equipment might be available for reservation only on Mondays, Tuesdays, and Wednesdays each week. You can set a resource-specific calendar to accurately represent when that resource is able to work on your project.

SHOW ME   Media 5.3—Understanding Resource Calendars
Access this video file through your registered Web Edition at my.safaribooksonline.com/9780132182461/media.

LET ME TRY IT

To set a separate calendar for a resource, follow these steps:

1. On the **Project** tab of the ribbon, in the **Properties** group, click **Change Working Time**.

2. Click **Create New Calendar**.

3. Choose how you want to create the resource's calendar:

   - **Create new base calendar**—Click this option to create a new calendar for the resource, from scratch. Working times will be set to the calendar options from the **Project Options** dialog box, by default.

- **Make a copy of [existing base] calendar**—Click this to use an existing base calendar as a starting point for the resource's calendar. Use the drop-down list to choose which base calendar you want to copy.

4. Type a name for the resource's calendar in the **Name** box. You may want to use a name that helps to identify this as a calendar that is intended for use by a specific resource. This helps differentiate it from the base and task calendars for your project.

5. Click **OK** to create the resource's calendar.

6. Similar to creating a base or task calendar, set the working days, nonworking days, default working times, and working times for specific time periods in the resource's calendar. For more information on these procedures, see the corresponding sections in Chapter 3, "Starting a Project."

7. With the resource's calendar set up and saved, on the **View** tab, in the **Resource Views** group, click **Resource Sheet**.

8. Choose the calendar you just created in the **Base Calendar** column for the corresponding resource.

Assigning Resources to Tasks

After you add resources to your project, the next step is to assign them to tasks within your project.

 LET ME TRY IT

Assigning a Resource Using the Task Information Dialog Box

You have a few different ways to assign work, material, and cost resources to tasks in your project. The Task Information dialog box provides a convenient location to identify details about the resource assignment, including the assignment owner and what percentage of the resource will be used for the task.

To assign a resource to a task in your project, follow these steps:

1. In the **Gantt Chart** view, double-click the row for a task.

2. Click the **Resources** tab on the **Task Information** dialog box.

3. Click once in the first available row in the **Resource Name** column and use the drop-down list to select the resource you're assigning to the task, as shown in Figure 5.1. This list is populated by the resources you have added to your project.

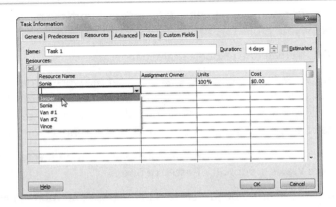

Figure 5.1   *Click the name of the resource you are assigning in the Resource Name column.*

If your organization has assignment owners who are separate from the project managers (for example, if your organization has a central resource manager for projects), type the resource's assignment owner in the **Assignment Owner** column. This is a rare, advanced situation.

4. Type a percentage in the **Units** column that represents how much of the resource's time (or, if you're assigning a material resource, units as identified in the **Material Label** column of the **Resource Sheet** view) will be spent on this task. For example, if a single resource is working half-time on this task and half-time on other tasks, type **50%** in the **Units** column.

The **Cost** column is automatically populated using the information you entered for the resource in the **Resource Sheet** view. To view the populated **Cost** column, click **OK** on the **Task Information** dialog box and then double-click the task again to reopen it and see the calculated cost.

5. Click **OK** to assign the resource to the task.

LET ME TRY IT

Assigning a Work Resource Using the Team Planner View

For work resources in your project, you can use the **Team Planner** view to assign tasks to specific people.

Here are the steps to follow to assign a task to a work resource using the **Team Planner** view:

1. On the **View** tab, in the **Resource Views** group, click **Team Planner**.

2. Click and drag a task listed under **Unassigned Tasks** up to a row in the time-scaled portion of the view for one of the work resources listed in the **Resource Name** column. When dragging the task, note that you can also adjust where the task falls horizontally in the time-scaled portion of the view. This will adjust the start and finish dates for the task and may result in a change in the constraint for the task.

3. If you want to add another resource to a task that is already assigned to a work resource in the **Team Planner** view, double-click the task bar to open the **Task Information** dialog box. Use the steps in the previous section, "Assigning a Resource Using the Task Information Dialog Box," to assign an additional resource.

Editing an Existing Resource Assignment

If resources in your project already have been assigned to tasks, it's possible that, at some point, you may need to make changes to those resource assignments. This isn't terribly complicated when work hasn't started on a task. Simply go back to the **Task Information** dialog box and make the necessary changes. This gets more complicated when a resource has started work on a task and the actual work values have been recorded in the project. You can take a few different approaches in this situation, depending on what changed:

- **If all work assigned to all resources on the task needs to pause and resume at a later time,** you can split the work on the task. This creates a gap between the first part of the task, in which the actual work has been recorded, and the next part of the task, in which the remaining work is scheduled.

- **If work assigned to one resource on the task needs to pause and resume at a later time,** you can use the **Resource Usage** view to fine-tune the work schedule for that resource.

- **If the remaining work assigned to one resource needs to be reassigned to another resource,** you can use the **Task Usage** view to move the remaining work to that resource.

SHOW ME   Media 5.4—Splitting a Task
Access this video file through your registered Web Edition at
my.safaribooksonline.com/9780132182461/media.

LET ME TRY IT

Splitting a Task to Create a Gap in Work

By splitting a task, you create a gap between one part of the task and another. This keeps the actual work where it was recorded but enables you to move the remaining work to a later time within the project schedule. When you split a task, all resource assignments for the task are split. If you just want to create a gap in one resource's schedule for the task, see the next section, "Fine-Tuning a Resource's Work Schedule for a Task."

To split work on a task, follow these steps:

1. In the **Gantt Chart** view, click the **Task** tab; in the **Schedule** group, click **Split Task,** as shown in Figure 5.2. The mouse cursor changes to a vertical line with an arrow pointing to the right.

Figure 5.2   *Click Split Task on the Task tab of the ribbon.*

2. On the Gantt bar for the task that you want to split, click the date when you want to end the work on the first part of the task and then drag the second part of the task to the date when you want work to resume. Figure 5.3 shows a task that has been split.

Figure 5.3 *This task has been split into two portions, with a gap in the middle represented by a dotted line.*

SHOW ME   Media 5.5—Using Usage Views to Edit Assignments
Access this video file through your registered Web Edition at my.safaribooksonline.com/9780132182461/media.

LET ME TRY IT

Fine-Tuning a Resource's Work Schedule for a Task

If a resource assigned to your task needs to put work on the task on hold for some reason (maybe to work on a last-minute, higher-priority task, for example), you can use the **Resource Usage** view to split that resource's work, without splitting the entire task.

Follow these steps to adjust the task's work schedule for a single resource:

1. On the **View** tab, in the **Resource Views** group, click **Resource Usage**.

2. On the **Format** tab, in the **Details** group, select the **Work** and **Actual Work** check boxes.

3. On the left portion of the **Resource Usage** view, scroll down to locate the resource that has an assignment you want to adjust, and then look below that resource for the task assignment. Scroll through the time-phased portion of the view, on the right side, to find the dates where work on the task is scheduled. Figure 5.4 shows an assignment with work in the time-phased portion of the view.

4. If the resource has recorded **Actual Work** on the task, the best practice is not to modify those hours. The **Work** row for the assignment contains the scheduled work. Any work that is scheduled for after the recorded **Actual Work** is fair game for moving. To move the scheduled work, delete the hours from each day when the resource will not be available and then retype the hours in the **Work** row for the assignment on the days when the resource can resume working on the task.

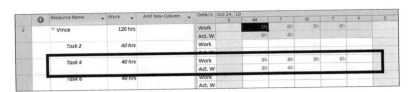

Figure 5.4 *This assignment has actual work reported on Monday and Tuesday, and scheduled work for Wednesday and Thursday.*

 **LET ME TRY IT**

Assigning Remaining Work on a Task to Another Resource

If a resource has been working on a task and recording actual work, but then is taken off of the task for some reason (poor performance or a job change, for example), you can move the remaining work to another resource.

To reassign the remaining work on a task to another resource, follow these steps:

1. In the **Gantt Chart** view, click the task that contains the resource you are replacing.

2. On the **Resource** tab, in the **Assignments** group, click **Assign Resources**.

3. On the **Assign Resources** dialog box, click the name of the resource you are replacing, and then click **Replace** (see Figure 5.5). Resources currently assigned to the selected task have a check mark displayed to the left of the **Resource Name** column.

4. On the **Replace Resource** dialog box, click the name of the resource you want to reassign work to, and then click **OK**.

5. Click **Close** on the **Assign Resources** dialog box.

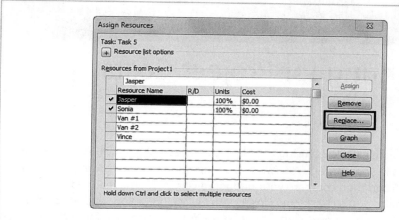

Figure 5.5 *Select a resource and click Replace.*

In this chapter, you learn about costs, budgets, and overtime in Project 2010.

6

Accounting for Project Costs

Project costs are calculated using the planned and actual work values for resource assignments in your project. You can also set up budgets within your project using Project 2010 and then compare your budgeted costs with the planned and actual costs. This helps you to track how closely you're sticking to your budget, so that you can determine the next steps, if necessary. You can also plan for and track overtime costs in your project using Project 2010.

Understanding Types of Costs

Project 2010 supports three different types of costs:

- **Rate-based costs**—These costs are incurred by a resource's pay rate (for example, an employee's hourly wages, or a daily rate for a machine rental).

- **Per-use costs**—These are one-time costs that may be incurred each time the resource is used within your project, or within a task in your project. For example, each time you rent a piece of equipment, there is an upfront per-use cost for the rental. It may be possible for a resource to have an associated per-use cost and rate-based cost.

- **Fixed costs**—These costs are associated with tasks, not resources, and they are incurred only once per task. For example, if a task in your project requires you to set up a temporary office in another location, the rent on that office space would be a fixed cost for that task.

These types of costs can be captured using work, material, and cost resources, as discussed in Chapter 5, "Working with Resources." Each resource can have an associated cost, and that cost is incurred when the resource is used within your project.

Note that these cost types are different from cost resources. Cost resources capture fees associated with getting tasks done, such as airfare or lodging. Rate-based, per-use, and fixed costs are associated with work and material resources, and are incurred based on when a resource is assigned to work, and how much work that resource completes.

SHOW ME   Media 6.1—Understand Types of Costs
Access this video file through your registered Web Edition at
my.safaribooksonline.com/9780132182461/media.

In addition to these cost types, Project also enables you to do some basic budgeting. You can provide some high-level budget figures and compare the actual costs incurred by tasks in your project with the budgeted costs you outlined during the planning process. The following section walks you through the budgeting process.

Creating a Budget for Your Project

Creating a project budget is a three-step process. First, you create budget resources and assign them to the project summary task, then you identify the budget values for the project (costs or number of hours), and finally, you match up each of your project's resources with a budget type, so you can compare budgeted values with actual values as your project progresses.

SHOW ME   Media 6.2—Set Up a Budget
Access this video file through your registered Web Edition at
my.safaribooksonline.com/9780132182461/media.

LET ME TRY IT

Creating and Assigning Budget Resources

The first step to creating a budget for your project is to create resources that represent each budget category in your organization. For example, your organization may have one budget for training costs and another budget for travel costs. To track these budgets in Project 2010, create two separate resources that represent each of these budgets in your project.

To create a budget resource, follow these steps:

1. On the **View** tab, in the **Resource Views** group, click **Resource Sheet**.

2. Type the name of the budget resource in the **Resource Name** column.

A best practice is to use a naming scheme that identifies the resource as a budget resource. For example, if I am adding a resource for my organization's training budget, I might choose to type **Budget-Training** in the **Resource Name** column.

3. Double-click the name of the budget resource to display the **Resource Information** dialog box.

4. Choose the resource type for the budget resource from the **Type** list.

5. Select the **Budget** check box, as shown in Figure 6.1.

6. Click **OK** to add the budget resource to your project.

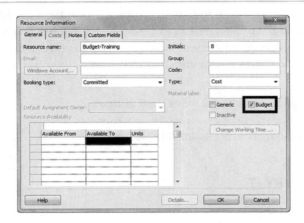

Figure 6.1 *The Budget check box appears below the Material Label field.*

After you create the resources, the next step is to assign them to the project summary task.

To assign a budget resource to the project summary task, follow these steps:

1. Click the **File** tab and then click **Options**.

2. Click **Advanced** on the left portion of the window.

3. Under **Display options for this project**, select the **Show project summary task** check box (shown in Figure 6.2), and then click **OK**.

4. On the **View** tab, in the **Task Views** group, click **Gantt Chart**.

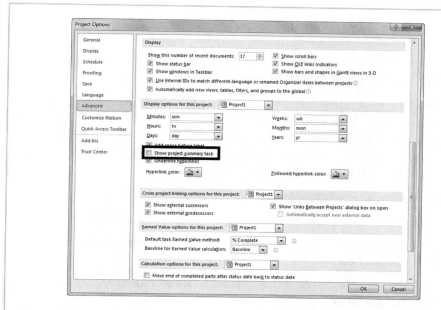

Figure 6.2   *The Show project summary task check box is highlighted.*

5. Double-click the first row in the **Gantt Chart** view to display the **Summary Task Information** dialog box for the project summary task.

6. Click the **Resources** tab and then select the budget resource from the drop-down list in the **Resource Name** column, as shown in Figure 6.3.

7. Click **OK** to assign the budget resource to the project summary task.

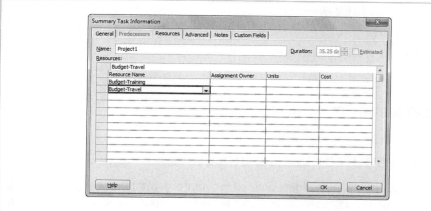

Figure 6.3   *Assigning the budget resources to the project summary task.*

LET ME TRY IT

Adding Values to Budget Resources

Right now, you have placeholders in your project for each budget in your organization, but we haven't identified values for those budgets. For example, if you added a resource called "Budget-Training," you've basically said that yes, there is a training budget, but you haven't said how much money there is in that budget. This is the next step in budgeting your project using Project 2010.

Follow these steps to provide values for your budget resources:

1. On the **View** tab, in **Resource Views** group, click **Resource Usage**.

2. Click the arrow on the right side of the **Add New Column** header and then click **Budget Cost**.

3. Click the arrow on the right side of the **Add New Column** header and then click **Budget Work**.

4. Scroll down in the left portion of the **Resource Usage** view to display the budget resources for your project. If your budget is measured as a cost, type the cost value for the budget in the **Budget Cost** column, as shown in Figure 6.4. If your budget is measured as an amount of work, type the work amount in the **Budget Work** column.

Resource Name ▾	Work ▾	Budget Cost ▾
⊟ Budget-Training		$100,000.00
Project1		$100,000.00
⊟ Budget-Travel		$300,000.00
Project1		$300,000.00

Figure 6.4   *These two budgets have assigned budget costs.*

LET ME TRY IT

Pairing Resources with Budgets

Now that you have your budgets defined for your organization, you can choose to go through each work, material, and cost resource in your project and give each a budget assignment. This step is not necessary for using budget resources, but it enables you to easily compare budgeted values against actual values as your project progresses. This comparison lets you see whether you're overspending, on track, or under-spending.

To match resources with budgets, follow these steps:

1. On the **View** tab, in **Resource Views** group, click **Resource Sheet**.

2. On the **Format** tab, in the **Columns** group, click **Custom Fields**.

3. Make sure that the **Resource** option is selected at the top of the **Custom Fields** dialog box, choose **Text** from the **Type** list, and then click **Text1** to select it.

4. Click **Rename**, type **Budget Assignment** in the **New name for 'Text1'** box, and then click **OK**.

5. Under **Calculation for assignment rows**, select **Roll down unless manually entered**, as shown in Figure 6.5.

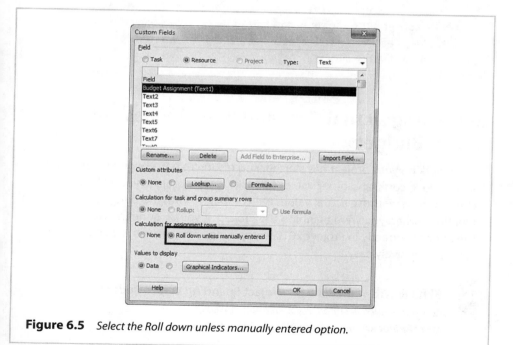

Figure 6.5   *Select the Roll down unless manually entered option.*

6. Click **OK** to finish defining the **Budget Assignment** custom field.

7. In the **Resource Sheet** view, click the arrow on the right side of the **Add New Column** header, and then click **Budget Assignment (Text1)**.

It may help to move the **Budget Assignment** column closer to the **Resource Name** column, so you can see easily which resources you're assigning to which budgets. To move the column after you add it, click the **Budget Assignment** column header once to select it. Now, when you hover over the column header, you see a four-way arrow. Click and drag the column header across the view to a spot closer to the **Resource Name** column.

8. In the **Budget Assignment** column for each resource in the **Resource Sheet** view, type the name of the budget to which you want the resource's actual values to be attributed. For example, if one of the resources in your project is a travel coordinator, you may want to attribute all costs that the travel coordinator incurs on your project to the **Travel** budget. Be sure to type values in the **Budget Assignment** column for each budget resource, as well.

Be sure to consistently type budget names in the **Budget Assignment** column. That is, be sure you use the same capitalization, spelling, spacing, and punctuation. This helps easily group resources later, when you want to compare actual values with budgeted values.

Comparing Actual Cost and Work Values with the Project Budget

After work on your project has started, and resources have begun recording the actual work, costs, and other values for tasks in your project, you'll likely want to check in on how those actual values are comparing with the budgeted values you identified when you were planning the project. If you've done the work to set up the budget correctly in Project 2010, comparing actual values with budgeted values is relatively easy.

 SHOW ME   Media 6.3—Project Spending Versus Budget
Access this video file through your registered Web Edition at
my.safaribooksonline.com/9780132182461/media.

LET ME TRY IT

To compare actual values with budgeted values, follow these steps:

1. On the **View** tab, in the **Resource Views** group, click **Resource Usage**.

2. On the **View** tab, in the **Data** group, click **Group by** and then click **New Group By**.

3. Type **Budget Assignment** in the **Name** box.

4. Click **Budget Assignment (Text1)** in the **Field Name** column for the **Group By** row, as shown in Figure 6.6.

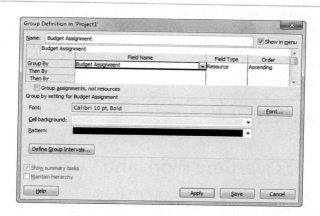

Figure 6.6   *Creating the Budget Assignment grouping for the Resource Usage view.*

5. Click **Apply**.

6. In the **Resource Usage** view, click the arrow on the right side of the **Add New Column** header and then click **Actual Cost**.

7. Click the arrow on the right side of the **Add New Column** header and then click **Actual Work**.

8. Compare the rolled-up values in the **Actual Cost** and **Actual Work** columns for each grouping with the rolled-up values in **Budget Cost** and **Budget Work**.

Accounting for Overtime Spent on Project Tasks

Overtime work isn't defined the same way in every organization. In some organizations, overtime is considered any work totaling more than 40 hours in one week. In other organizations, overtime is considered any work beyond eight hours in one day. Overtime sometimes is calculated on a monthly basis, and other times, extra hours don't count as overtime costs because the resources are salaried. Even within one organization, there may not be a single hard-and-fast rule about overtime. Some resources may be salaried; other resources may record overtime on a daily basis; and others may account for overtime weekly.

Because of this, Project makes no assumptions about overtime. If a resource reports that he or she has worked 10 hours in one day, Project records those 10 hours as regular work. It's up to the project manager to determine whether two of those 10 hours are actually overtime work. After the project manager has manually changed the reported work to eight hours of regular work and two hours of overtime work, the overtime rate for the resource will apply for those two hours, and costs will be accounted for correctly.

 **LET ME TRY IT**

Planning for Overtime Work and Costs

If you know that some of the work on your project will be done as overtime work, you can plan for that overtime work before it actually happens. This enables you to more accurately estimate project costs by including overtime rates for resources during the planning process.

Follow these steps to plan for overtime work in Project 2010:

1. On the **View** tab, in the **Task Views** group, click **Task Usage**.

2. On the **View** tab, in the **Data** group, click **Tables** and then click **Work**.

3. On the left portion of the **Task Usage** view, click the **Add New Column** header and then click **Overtime Work**.

4. Type the amount of overtime you want to plan for in the **Overtime Work** column for an italicized resource assignment, as shown in Figure 6.7.

Overtime work is considered part of the total work for a resource assignment. If the resource assignment is set to 40 hours of work, and you add 10 hours in the **Overtime Work** column, the **Work** column will stay set to 40 hours. If you meant to indicate that those 10 hours would be in addition to the existing 40 hours, you need to adjust the **Work** column to add the overtime (50 hours of work). Project calculates costs as follows:

(Overtime Work × Overtime Rate) = Overtime Cost

[(Work − Overtime Work) × Standard Rate] + Overtime Cost + Fixed Costs + Costs Per Use = Cost

Task Name	Work	Overtime Work
⊟ **Phase 2**	**230 hrs**	**10 hrs**
⊟ Task 4	50 hrs	10 hrs
Vince	50 hrs	10 hrs

Figure 6.7   *Adding planned overtime to a resource assignment.*

LET ME TRY IT

Recording Actual Overtime Work and Costs

As resources on your project begin work on tasks, their actual work hours will begin rolling in. As the project manager, you'll need to be recording how much of each resource's time is actually overtime.

To add actual overtime work to your project, follow these steps:

1. On the **View** menu, in the **Task Views** group, click **Task Usage**.

2. On the **View** tab, in the **Data** group, click **Tables** and then click **Work**.

3. On the **Format** tab, in the **Details** group, click **Add Details**.

4. In the **Available fields** box, click **Actual Overtime Work** and then press **Ctrl** and click **Actual Work**.

5. Click **Show** to move the selected fields to the **Show these fields** box.

6. Click **Actual Work** in the **Show these fields** box to select it and then click the up arrow button on the right side of the box to move the **Actual Work** field above the **Actual Overtime Work** field.

7. Click **OK** to add these fields to the time-phased (right) portion of the **Task Usage** view.

8. Scroll through the list of tasks and resource assignments to display the resource assignment that has overtime and then click the row header to select the row.

9. On the **View** tab, in the **Zoom** group, click **Zoom Selected Tasks**, as shown in Figure 6.8.

Figure 6.8   *Click Zoom Selected Tasks in the Zoom group on the View tab.*

10. For each resource assignment, look at the **Actual Work** row in the time-phased portion of the view and watch for reported work that exceeds the resource's standard amount of work. For example, look at Figure 6.9. The highlighted resource normally works eight hour days, and I see 10 hours of actual work reported in one day, so I know that resource has worked some overtime on that day, according to company policy.

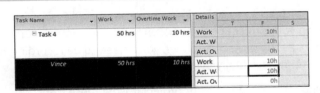

Figure 6.9   *This resource normally works eight hour days, so this 10-hour day includes overtime work.*

11. Determine how much of the reported **Actual Work** is overtime work and subtract that from the work total. For example, if my resource reported 10 hours of work, I know that two of those hours are overtime, so I subtract 2 from 10 to get eight hours.

12. Type the new work total, minus the overtime work, in the corresponding cell in the **Actual Work** row.

13. In the corresponding **Actual Overtime Work** row, type the amount of overtime work that the resource reported and then press **Enter**. The **Actual Work** row will be updated to add back the overtime work.

After the actual overtime work has been correctly recorded in your project, the resource's overtime rate will be used to calculate the overtime costs.

This chapter discusses how you can use Project 2010 to capture what's going on in your project and how to compare it to what you had planned.

7

Capturing Project Progress

As resources on your project begin work on tasks, they will have actual work hours and status to report. If your organization uses Project Professional 2010 with Project Server, some of this reporting is streamlined. However, you can choose to collect progress through more traditional means, such as weekly status reports and team meetings. If you go this route, you'll need to manually enter progress into Project 2010.

Baselining Your Project

After your project is initially set up, it can be helpful to set a project baseline. A *baseline* is a snapshot of your project data, including dates, durations, work estimates, and cost estimates. By baselining your project, you capture your project plan so that later, as your project progresses, you can compare what's actually going on in your project with what you had initially planned.

You can also set separate baselines at certain points in your project, such as milestones and stage gates, for example. Project 2010 enables you to set up to 11 different baselines in each project.

 LET ME TRY IT

To set a baseline in your project, follow these steps:

1. In the **Gantt Chart** view, press **Ctrl** and click each row header for the tasks you want to baseline. If you want to baseline the whole project, skip this step.

2. On the **Project** tab, in the **Schedule** group, click **Set Baseline** and then click **Set Baseline** on the menu that appears.

3. Click **Set Baseline** and then choose the baseline number that you want to set from the drop-down list, as shown in Figure 7.1.

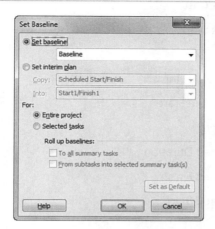

Figure 7.1   *Use the Set Baseline dialog box to choose baseline options.*

If you need to capture only the start and finish dates for the project or the selected tasks, you can use an interim plan instead of a baseline. Click **Set interim plan**, choose which date fields you want to **Copy**, and then, from the **Into** list, choose the interim plan number where you want to capture the selected dates.

4. Under **For**, click **Entire project** if you want to set the baseline for the project or click **Selected tasks** if you want to copy only the tasks you selected in the **Gantt Chart** view.

5. If you chose **Selected tasks**, under **Roll up baselines**, select the appropriate options:

    *   **To all summary tasks**—Select this check box if you want the baselined data to be rolled up to the summary task level for all tasks, regardless of whether you selected the summary tasks for baselining.

    *   **From subtasks into selected summary task(s)**—Select this check box if you want only baseline data to be rolled up to summary tasks that you selected in the **Gantt Chart** view.

6. Click **OK** to set the baseline in your project.

With a baseline set, you can start work in your project and then use the baseline fields to compare data later in your project's timeline. Baseline fields include the following:

- Baseline Budget Cost
- Baseline Budget Work
- Baseline Cost
- Baseline Deliverable Finish
- Baseline Deliverable Start
- Baseline Duration
- Baseline Estimated Duration
- Baseline Estimated Finish
- Baseline Estimated Start
- Baseline Finish
- Baseline Fixed Cost
- Baseline Fixed Cost Accrual
- Baseline Start
- Baseline Work

Gathering Status Updates from Resources

Resources should be periodically reporting their task work and status, either using Project Server or through other means, such as weekly status reports or meetings. If your organization uses Project Professional 2010 with Project Server, resource time and task status will be captured by the resource in Project Server and then submitted to an approver who can accept or reject it. Accepted time and status are added to the project, and the actual data within your project will be updated.

If your organization does not use Project Server, you need to ask for time and task status regularly and manually add that actual data to your project. Let's say you have a task in your project that has a two-week duration, with two resources assigned at 80 hours each. Those resources provide you with status updates in email, which you manually enter into Project. The resources need to provide you with one of three different "packages" of status information:

- Actual start, percent work complete, and remaining work
- Actual start, actual work, remaining work, and an expected finish date
- Day-by-day timesheet of actual work per day, remaining work, and an expected finish date

The following sections walk you through what each of these options include, and where to enter the status information in Project, to get an accurate look at how your project is progressing.

Actual Start, Percent Work Complete, Remaining Work

This method of manually recording status is the fastest, but it is also likely the least accurate. With this method, resources provide you with the following:

- **Actual Start**—This is the date when the resource actually began working on the task.

- **Percent (%) Work Complete**—The **% Work Complete** field is used to capture approximately how much work has been done on a task, as a percentage.

- **Remaining Work**—This is the estimated amount of work that is left to be done on the task.

Using the earlier example, Figure 7.2 shows a task with a two-week duration (10 days), with two resources assigned at 80 hours each. Notice that the task is scheduled to start on 2/21/11 and finish on 3/4/11.

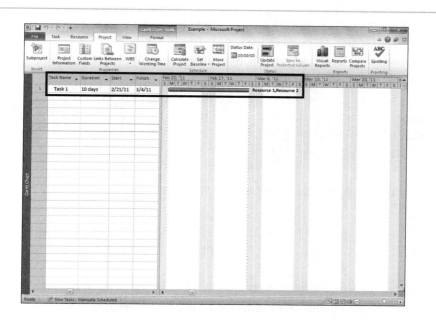

Figure 7.2   *An example of a two-week task with two assigned resources*

On 2/25/11, half way through the scheduled duration, the two assigned resources provide the following information:

- **Resource 1**—Began work on the task on 2/21/11, currently about 50% complete, with about 40 more hours of work left to do.

- **Resource 2**—Began work on the task on 2/22/11, currently about 60% complete, with about 20 hours of work left to do.

SHOW ME   Media 7.1—Entering Actual Start, % Work Complete, and Remaining Work
Access this video file through your registered Web Edition at my.safaribooksonline.com/9780132182461/media.

LET ME TRY IT

To enter resource status data in Project, you first need to display the corresponding fields, using the following steps:

1. On the **View** tab, in the **Resource Views** group, click **Resource Usage**.

2. Click the **Add New Column** header, and add the **Actual Start** column. Repeat this to add the **% Work Complete** and **Remaining Work** columns.

With these fields displayed, now you can add the status information you received from the resources assigned to the task. This status information is entered in the assignment row for the task, in the **Resource Usage** view. Assignment rows are indented below each resource's name.

You can also use the **Task Usage** view to enter assignment data. Add the same fields to the **Task Usage** view, and enter assignment data for each resource indented below the task name.

First, add the information from Resource 1, as shown in Figure 7.3.

Resource Name	Work	Actual Start	% Work Complete	Remaining Work
⊟ Resource 1	80 hrs	NA	50%	40 hrs
Task 1	80 hrs	2/21/11	50%	40 hrs
⊟ Resource 2	80 hrs	NA	0%	80 hrs
Task 1	80 hrs	NA	0%	80 hrs

Figure 7.3   *The Resource Usage view, with status data from Resource 1 added*

To add status data from a resource, follow these steps:

1. On the **View** tab, in the **Resource Views** group, click **Resource Usage**.

2. Enter the date that the resource actually began working on the task in the **Actual Start** column for the task assignment.

3. Type the percentage of work that the resource thinks has been completed in the **% Work Complete** column. Project will calculate the remaining work, based on the scheduled work and the percentage you entered here.

4. If the amount of remaining work that Project calculated is different from the remaining work reported by the resource, type the data reported by the resource in the **Remaining Work** column. Notice that the **% Work Complete** column is adjusted to show the accurate percentage, based on the scheduled work and the remaining work you entered here.

If you go back to the **Gantt Chart** view and take a look, you'll see a progress bar added over the Gantt bar for the task, representing how far along the task is, with just Resource 1's status data added (shown in Figure 7.4).

Task Name	Duration	Start	Finish	Feb 20, '11	Feb 27, '11	Mar 6, '11
				S M T W T F S	S M T W T F S	S M T W T F S
Task 1	10 days	2/21/11	3/4/11			Resource 1,Resource 2

Figure 7.4 *The Gantt Chart view, after adding status data from Resource 1*

Next, you need to go back to the **Resource Usage** view and add in the status data provided by Resource 2, as shown in Figure 7.5.

Resource Name	Work	Actual Start	% Work Complete	Remaining Work
⊟ Resource 1	80 hrs	NA	50%	40 hrs
Task 1	80 hrs	2/21/11	50%	40 hrs
⊟ Resource 2	68 hrs	NA	71%	20 hrs
Task 1	68 hrs	2/22/11	71%	20 hrs

Figure 7.5 *The Resource Usage view, with status data from Resource 2 added*

Let's take a closer look at the calculations going on here. In the example, Resource 2 has 80 hours of scheduled work. He reports that he is about 60% complete, with about 20 hours of work remaining on the task. When you enter this resource's percent work complete, Project begins by calculating how much **Actual Work** has been completed, using this formula:

% Work Complete = (Actual Work / Work) * 100

So, in this example, Project uses the following equation to calculate **Actual Work**:

60% = (Actual Work / 80h) * 100

Begin by dividing both sides of the equation by 100:

60% / 100 = [(Actual Work / 80h) * 100] / 100

This trims down the equation to the following:

.6 = Actual Work / 80h

Then multiply both sides by 80 to solve for **Actual Work**:

.6 * 80 = (Actual Work / 80h) * 80

This leaves you with the **Actual Work** value:

48h = Actual Work

Once Project has calculated the **Actual Work**, the next step is to calculate **Remaining Work**, using the following formula:

Remaining Work = Work - Actual Work

In this example, the following equation is used:

Remaining Work = 80h - 48h

The resulting value for the **Remaining Work** column is 32 hours of work remaining on the task.

However, recall that one of the values that the resource provided in his status report was an estimate of the remaining work on the task, and that estimate was 20 hours. At this point, you need to decide which you think is more accurate: the resource's estimate on what percentage of the work is complete, or the resource's estimate on how many hours it will take to complete the task. If you think the resource's remaining work estimate is more accurate, enter that in the **Remaining Work** column, and Project will recalculate the **% Work Complete** value, using the formulas we just walked through.

Now, let's go back and look at the task in the **Gantt Chart** view, with status data from both resources added (shown in Figure 7.6). The vertical line shows the current date, and the progress bar extends beyond that date, indicating that this task is ahead of schedule.

Figure 7.6   *The Gantt Chart view, after adding status data from Resource 2*

You can quickly set tasks to 0%, 25%, 50%, 75%, or 100% complete by selecting a task and then clicking the corresponding buttons on the **Task** tab, in the **Schedule** group. Clicking these buttons sets the **Percent Complete** and **Percent Work Complete** fields to the corresponding value.

After you add the actual start, percent work complete, and remaining work provided by the resources assigned to a task, a best practice is to reevaluate the finish date for the task. The status data you just entered may have pushed the finish date for the task out, or made it possible to shorten the duration and get the task done sooner. These changes may have an impact on other tasks in your project, or even on other projects that are dependent on your project: Actual Start, Actual Work, Remaining Work, Expected Finish Date.

This method of recording status requires that resources provide you with the following:

- **Actual Start**—This is the date when the resource actually began working on the task.

- **Actual Work**—This is the number of hours a resource has currently put in on the task.

- **Remaining Work**—This is the estimated amount of work that is left to be done on the task.

- **Expected Finish Date**—This is the resource's best guess for a date when the task will be completed.

You can capture this status information in the **Resource Usage** or **Task Usage** view. The previous section used the **Resource Usage** view, so this section walks through using the **Task Usage** view to enter assignment information.

Returning to the previous example, you are managing a project with a task that has a 10-day duration, with two resources assigned at 80 hours each.

On 2/25/11, half way through the scheduled duration, the two assigned resources provide the following information:

- **Resource 1**—Began work on the task on 2/21/11, completed 40 hours of work, about 40 more hours of work left to do, estimated finish of 3/4/11.

- **Resource 2**—Began work on the task on 2/22/11, completed 48 hours of work, about 20 hours of work left to do, estimated finish of 3/2/11.

SHOW ME   Media 7.2—Entering Actual Start, Actual Work, Remaining Work, and Finish Date
Access this video file through your registered Web Edition at
my.safaribooksonline.com/9780132182461/media.

LET ME TRY IT

To enter resource status data in Project, first you need to display the corresponding fields, using the following steps:

1. On the **View** tab, in the **Task Views** group, click **Task Usage**.

2. Click the **Add New Column** header, and add the **Actual Start** column. Repeat this to add the **Actual Work, Remaining Work**, and **Finish** columns.

With these fields displayed, now you can add the status information you received from the resources assigned to the task. This status information is entered in the assignment row for the task, in the **Task Usage** view. Assignment rows are indented below each task's name. If you are using the **Resource Usage** view, assignment rows are indented below each resource's name.

First, add the information from Resource 1, as shown in Figure 7.7.

Task Name	Actual Start	Actual Work	Remaining Work	Finish
Task 1	2/21/11	40 hrs	120 hrs	3/4/11
Resource 1	2/21/11	40 hrs	40 hrs	3/4/11
Resource 2	NA	0 hrs	80 hrs	3/4/11

Figure 7.7   *The Task Usage view, with status data from Resource 1 added*

To add status data from a resource, follow these steps:

1. On the **View** tab, in the **Task Views** group, click **Task Usage**.

2. Enter the date that the resource actually began working on the task in the **Actual Start** column for the assignment.

3. Type the amount of work that the resource has completed on the task in the **Actual Work** column for the assignment. Project will calculate the remaining work, based on the scheduled work and the actual work value you entered here.

4. If the amount of remaining work that Project calculated is different from the remaining work reported by the resource, type the data reported by the resource in the **Remaining Work** column.

5. Enter the estimated finish date for the task in the **Finish** column for the assignment, if necessary.

Repeat this to add in the status data provided by Resource 2. Notice that after adding the 20 hours of remaining work, when you add the estimated **Finish** date of 3/2/11, the **Remaining Work** column is adjusted. This is because Project is assuming that the resource worked 8-hour days. To correct this, you can use the right, timephased portion of the **Task Usage** view, as shown in Figure 7.8.

Task Name	Details	Feb 20, '11							Feb 27, '11
		S	M	T	W	T	F	S	S
⊟ Task 1	Work		8h	16h	16h	16h	16h		
	Act. W		8h	16h	16h	16h	16h		
Resource 1	Work		8h	8h	8h	8h	8h		
	Act. W		8h	8h	8h	8h	8h		
Resource 2	Work		0h	8h	8h	8h	8h		
	Act. W		0h	8h	8h	8h	8h		

Figure 7.8   *The right portion of the Task Usage view spreads the work values across a timeline.*

To adjust actual work values in the timephased portion of the **Task Usage** view, follow these steps:

1. On the **View** tab, in the **Task Views** group, click **Task Usage**.

2. On the **Format** tab, in the **Details** group, select the **Actual Work** check box. This adds rows to capture actual work in the timephased portion of the **Task Usage** view.

3. Adjust the values in the **Actual Work** row for the assignment, to reflect the accurate hours spent on the task.

In the example, because Project assumed the resource was working 8-hour days, the timephased data shows six 8-hour days (totaling 48 hours), when the resource actually worked four 12-hour days. Figure 7.9 shows what the timephased data looks like initially.

Figure 7.10 shows the corrected timephased data.

After the timephased data is corrected, the **Finish** column reflects the resource's reported estimated finish date for the task, as shown in Figure 7.11.

Task Name ▾	Details	Feb 20, '11							Feb 27, '11			
		S	M	T	W	T	F	S	S	M	T	W
⊟ Task 1	Work		8h	16h	16h	16h	16h			16h	16h	16h
	Act. W		8h	16h	16h	16h	16h			8h	8h	
Resource 1	Work		8h	8h	8h	8h	8h			8h	8h	8h
	Act. W		8h	8h	8h	8h	8h					
Resource 2	Work		0h	8h	8h	8h	8h			8h	8h	8h
	Act. W		0h	8h	8h	8h	8h			8h	8h	

Figure 7.9   *Timephased data in the Task Usage view, before correction.*

Task Name ▾	Details	Feb 20, '11							Feb 27, '11			
		S	M	T	W	T	F	S	S	M	T	W
⊟ Task 1	Work		8h	20h	20h	20h	20h			16h	16h	12h
	Act. W		8h	20h	20h	20h	20h					
Resource 1	Work		8h	8h	8h	8h	8h			8h	8h	8h
	Act. W		8h	8h	8h	8h	8h					
Resource 2	Work		0h	12h	12h	12h	12h			8h	8h	4h
	Act. W		0h	12h	12h	12h	12h					

Figure 7.10   *Timephased data in the Task Usage view, after correction.*

Task Name ▾	Actual Start ▾	Actual Work ▾	Remaining Work ▾	Finish ▾
⊟ Task 1	2/21/11	88 hrs	60 hrs	3/4/11
Resource 1	2/21/11	40 hrs	40 hrs	3/4/11
Resource 2	2/22/11	48 hrs	20 hrs	3/2/11

Figure 7.11   *Reported resource status data, after correcting timephased data.*

Actual Work Per Day, Remaining Work, Expected Finish Date

This method of recording status requires that resources provide you with the following:

- **Actual Work Per Day**—This is a day-by-day breakdown, in the form of a timesheet, for the work that the resource has actually completed on the task. For example, 8 hours on Monday, 7 hours on Tuesday, 9 hours on Wednesday, and so on.

- **Remaining Work**—This is the estimated amount of work that is left to be done on the task.

- **Expected Finish Date**—This is the resource's best guess for a date when the task will be completed.

Because the resources are providing a day-by-day account of actual work, they do not need to provide the actual start date separately. The first day of actual work provided in the day-by-day account of work is the actual start date.

You can capture this status information in the **Resource Usage** or **Task Usage** view.

Returning to the previous example, recall that you are managing a project with a task that has a 10-day duration, with two resources assigned at 80 hours each.

On 2/25/11, half way through the scheduled duration, the two assigned resources provide the following information:

- **Resource 1**

  - Day-by-day breakdown of work, as detailed in the following table:

Monday	Tuesday	Wednesday	Thursday	Friday
8h	8h	8h	8h	8h

  - About 40 more hours of work left to do
  - Estimated finish of 3/4/11

- **Resource 2**

  - Day-by-day breakdown of work, as detailed in the following table:

Monday	Tuesday	Wednesday	Thursday	Friday
0h	12h	12h	12h	12h

  - About 20 hours of work left to do
  - Estimated finish of 3/2/11

 SHOW ME   Media 7.3—Entering Actual Work Per Day, Remaining Work, and Finish Date
Access this video file through your registered Web Edition at my.safaribooksonline.com/9780132182461/media.

LET ME TRY IT

To enter resource status data in Project, first you need to set up the Resource Usage or Task Usage view, using the following steps:

1. On the **View** tab, in the **Resource Views** group, click **Resource Usage**. Or, if you want to use the **Task Usage** view, on the **View** tab, in the **Task Views** group, click **Task Usage**.

2. Click the **Add New Column** header, and add the **Remaining Work** column. Repeat this to add the **Finish** column.

3. On the **Format** tab, in the **Details** group, select the **Actual Work** check box.

With the **Resource Usage** or **Task Usage** view set up, now you can add the status information you received from the resources assigned to the task. This status information is entered in the corresponding assignment row. In the **Resource Usage** view, assignment rows are indented below each resource's name. In the **Task Usage** view, assignment rows are indented below each task's name.

First, add the information from Resource 1, as shown in Figure 7.12.

Resource Name	Work	Remaining Work	Finish	Details	Feb 20, '11						
---	---	---	---	---	S	M	T	W	T	F	S
⊟ Resource 1	80 hrs	40 hrs	3/4/11	Work		8h	8h	8h	8h	8h	
				Act. W		8h	8h	8h	8h	8h	
Task 1	80 hrs	40 hrs	3/4/11	Work		8h	8h	8h	8h	8h	
				Act. W		8h	8h	8h	8h	8h	
⊟ Resource 2	80 hrs	80 hrs	3/4/11	Work		8h	8h	8h	8h	8h	
				Act. W							
Task 1	80 hrs	80 hrs	3/4/11	Work		8h	8h	8h	8h	8h	
				Act. W							

Figure 7.12   *The Resource Usage view, with status data from Resource 1 added*

To add status data from a resource, follow these steps:

1. On the **View** tab, in the **Resource Views** group, click **Resource Usage**. Or, if you want to use the **Task Usage** view, on the **View** tab, in the **Task Views** group, click **Task Usage**.

2. Enter the day-by-day hours that the resource spent on the task in the **Actual Work** assignment row of the right, timephased portion of the view, as shown in Figure 7.13.

3. If the amount of remaining work that Project calculated is different from the remaining work reported by the resource, type the data reported by the resource in the **Remaining Work** column.

Resource Name	Work	Remaining Work	Finish	Details	Feb 20, '11					
					S	M	T	W	T	F	S
− Resource 1	80 hrs	40 hrs	3/4/11	Work		8h	8h	8h	8h	8h	
				Act. W		8h	8h	8h	8h	8h	
Task 1	80 hrs	40 hrs	3/4/11	Work		8h	8h	8h	8h	8h	
				Act. W		8h	8h	8h	8h	8h	
− Resource 2	80 hrs	80 hrs	3/4/11	Work		8h	8h	8h	8h	8h	
				Act. W							
Task 1	80 hrs	80 hrs	3/4/11	Work		8h	8h	8h	8h	8h	
				Act. W							

Figure 7.13   *Day-by-day hours entered in the Actual Work row for the assignment*

4. Enter the estimated finish date for the task in the **Finish** column for the assignment, if necessary.

Repeat this to add in the status data provided by Resource 2, as shown in Figure 7.14.

Resource Name	Work	Remaining Work	Finish	Details	Feb 20, '11					
					S	M	T	W	T	F	S
− Resource 1	80 hrs	40 hrs	3/4/11	Work		8h	8h	8h	8h	8h	
				Act. W		8h	8h	8h	8h	8h	
Task 1	80 hrs	40 hrs	3/4/11	Work		8h	8h	8h	8h	8h	
				Act. W		8h	8h	8h	8h	8h	
− Resource 2	68 hrs	20 hrs	3/2/11	Work		0h	12h	12h	12h	12h	
				Act. W		0h	12h	12h	12h	12h	
Task 1	68 hrs	20 hrs	3/2/11	Work		0h	12h	12h	12h	12h	
				Act. W		0h	12h	12h	12h	12h	

Figure 7.14   *The Resource Usage view, with status data from Resource 2 added*

Assessing the Impacts of Updates

As your project is updated with actual data, the dates of other, linked tasks in your project will be affected. For example, if Task B can't start until Task A finishes, and Task A finishes late, the start of Task B will be delayed. The series of linked tasks in your project that determine the start and finish dates for your entire project are referred to as the *critical path*. You can view the critical path in Project by using the Tracking Gantt view.

SHOW ME   Media 7.4—Understanding the Critical Path
Access this video file through your registered Web Edition at
my.safaribooksonline.com/9780132182461/media.

LET ME TRY IT

To display the critical path in the Tracking Gantt view, follow these steps:

1. On the **View** tab, in the **Task Views** group, click **Other Views** and then click **More Views**.

2. In the **Views** box, click **Tracking Gantt** and then click **Apply**.

3. On the **View** tab, in the **Zoom** group, click **Entire Project**. Gantt bars for tasks on the critical path for your project appear in red.

Displaying the critical path lets you see whether updates made to your project have changed your project's finish date, or other important milestones. If you find that updates have adversely affected the project schedule, you can get more detail about what's driving the dates using the Task Inspector pane, which shows the factors that are driving the schedule for a selected task, such as whether the task is manually or automatically scheduled, what the start/finish dates and actual start/finish dates are, relevant resource information, what constraints are applied, and other factors.

Follow these steps to display the Task Inspector pane:

1. On the **Task** tab, in the **Tasks** group, click **Inspect**.

2. Click a task in the currently displayed view to see details about that task in the **Task Inspector** pane. Figure 7.15 shows an example.

Figure 7.15   *The Task Inspector pane.*

This chapter includes information on reporting, sharing project details, and collaborating on a project using Project 2010.

8

Sharing Your Project with Others

Projects rarely are created and managed by one person in a small room with no outside influence. Project managers have supervisors that they need to report to about project status, other interested parties who want access to project data, and other project managers who may have some insight into ways to improve project plans. Project 2010 enables reporting, other sharing methods, and a collaboration system to support coordinating project management work with outside demands for project information.

 SHOW ME Media 8.1—Sharing Your Project
Access this video file through your registered Web Edition at
my.safaribooksonline.com/9780132182461/media.

Reporting on Your Project

Project 2010 includes two types of reports:

- **Visual reports**—When you generate a visual report, your project data is exported to Excel or Visio, for a highly illustrated report that takes advantage of PivotTable and PivotChart features.

- **Basic reports**—When you generate a basic report, your project data is formatted into a simple, printable report within Project 2010.

Figure 8.1 shows an example of a report generated using visual reports and Figure 8.2 shows a similar one generated using basic reports.

With both visual and basic reports, not only can you generate them using your project data, but you can also customize your own reports to show the data you need, in the way that makes the most sense for your organization. The process for generating and customizing reports is different based on which kind of report you are using.

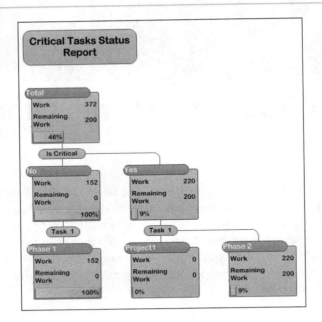

Figure 8.1   *The Critical Tasks Status Report, a visual report that uses Visio*

ID	Indicators			Task Mode	Task Name	Duration	Start	Finish
					Critical Tasks as of 9/5/10 11:26 PM			
					Project1			
5				Auto Schedule	Phase 2	21.25 days	10/22/10 8:00 AM	11/22/10 10:00 AM
6				Auto Schedule	Task 4	5 days	10/22/10 3:00 AM	10/28/10 5:00 PM
	ID	Successor Name	Type	Lag				
	7	Task 5	FS	0 days				
7				Auto Schedule	Task 5	3.75 days	10/29/10 8:00 AM	11/3/10 3:00 PM
	ID	Successor Name	Type	Lag				
	8	Task 6	FS	0 days				
8				Auto Schedule	Task 6	5 days	11/3/10 3:00 PM	11/10/10 3:00 PM
	ID	Successor Name	Type	Lag				
	9	Task 7	FS	-50%				
9				Auto Schedule	Task 7	5 days	11/8/10 10:00 AM	11/15/10 10:00 AM
	ID	Successor Name	Type	Lag				
	10	Task 8	FS	0 days				
10				Auto Schedule	Task 8	5 days	11/15/10 10:00 AM	11/22/10 10:00 AM

Figure 8.2   *The Critical Tasks basic report*

 **LET ME TRY IT**

Generating and Customizing a Visual Report

Project 2010 comes with the visual report templates shown in Table 8.1.

Table 8.1 Available Visual Reports

Excel	Visio
Baseline Cost Report	Baseline Report
Baseline Work Report	Cash Flow Report
Budget Cost Report	Critical Tasks Status Report
Budget Work Report	Critical Tasks Status Report
Cash Flow Report	Resource Availability Report
Earned Value Over Time Report	Resource Status Report
Resource Cost Summary Report	Task Status Report
Resource Remaining Work Report	
Resource Work Availability Report	
Resource Work Summary Report	

Follow these steps to generate one of these visual reports:

1. On the **Project** tab, in the **Reports** group, click **Visual Reports**.

2. Click the name of the report you want to generate.

> To narrow down the list of reports, you can click each tab on the **Visual Reports—Create Report** dialog box to view only reports that fit each category (such as **Task Usage** or **Resource Summary**, for example). You can also choose to display only reports that open in Excel or only those that open in Visio, by selecting or clearing the **Microsoft Excel** and **Microsoft Visio** check boxes. This filters the list of reports by whichever application you select.

3. To choose the amount of usage detail you want to include in the report, select an option from the **Select level of usage data to include in the report** list.

A best practice is to leave the usage detail set to whatever Project uses as the default. In most cases, this will be **Weeks**. Including more detail (**Days**, for example) may impact the performance of the report. If the report you are generating doesn't need to include usage data, choose **Years** to get the best level of performance for the report.

4. Click **View** to begin generating the report. Based on your selection, the report will open in Excel or Visio, and you can modify what data is displayed by using the PivotTable or PivotChart features within those applications.

If the default visual report templates included with Project 2010 don't include the right data to meet your needs, you can add or remove which fields are included in the report.

To add or remove fields from an existing visual report template, follow these steps:

1. On the **Project** tab, in the **Reports** group, click **Visual Reports**.

2. Click the name of the report you want to modify and then click **Edit Template**. The **Visual Reports—Field Picker** dialog box appears, as shown in Figure 8.3.

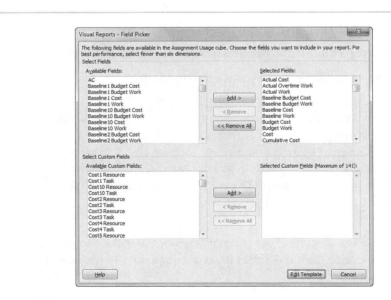

Figure 8.3 *Use the Visual Reports—Field Picker dialog box to choose fields to include in the selected report.*

3. To add a built-in Project field to the report, under **Select Fields**, click the name of the field in the **Available Fields** box and then click **Add** to move it to the **Selected Fields** box.

4. To remove a built-in Project field from the report, under **Select Fields**, click the name of the field in the **Selected Fields** box and then click **Remove** to move it to the **Available Fields** box.

5. To add a custom field to the report, under **Select Custom Fields**, click the name of the field in the **Available Custom Fields** box and then click **Add** to move it to the **Selected Custom Fields** box.

6. To remove a custom field from the report, under **Select Custom Fields**, click the name of the field in the **Selected Custom Fields** box, and then click **Remove** to move it to the **Available Custom Fields** box.

7. Click **Edit Template**, and the template opens in Excel or Visio. Use the features in the application to surface the data you added or to rearrange the report to account for the data you removed.

If the existing reports don't come anywhere near meeting your needs, you can create your own report by choosing what format you want to use and what data you want to export.

To create a new visual report template, follow these steps:

1. On the **Project** tab, in the **Reports** group, click **Visual Reports**.

2. Click **New Template**.

3. Under **Select Application**, choose whether you want to create the report in Excel or Visio.

4. Under **Select Data Type**, choose a category of usage or summary data that includes the information you want in your report.

5. Under **Select Fields**, click **Field Picker**.

6. To add a built-in Project field to the report, under **Select Fields**, click the name of the field in the **Available Fields** box, and then click **Add** to move it to the **Selected Fields** box.

7. To remove a built-in Project field from the report, under **Select Fields**, click the name of the field in the **Selected Fields** box, and then click **Remove** to move it to the **Available Fields** box.

8. To add a custom field to the report, under **Select Custom Fields**, click the name of the field in the **Available Custom Fields** box, and then click **Add** to move it to the **Selected Custom Fields** box.

9. To remove a custom field from the report, under **Select Custom Fields**, click the name of the field in the **Selected Custom Fields** box, and then click **Remove** to move it to the **Available Custom Fields** box.

10. Click **OK** on the **Visual Reports—Field Picker** dialog box to add the selected fields to the report.

11. Click **OK** on the **Visual Reports—New Template** dialog box to export the data to Excel or Visio and begin designing the visual layout of your report. Use the PivotTable and PivotChart features in those applications to choose how you want to present your project data.

Generating and Customizing a Basic Report

Table 8.2 shows the basic reports included in Project 2010.

Table 8.2   Available Basic Reports

Category	Report Name
Overview	Project Summary
	Top-Level Tasks
	Critical Tasks
	Milestones
	Working Days
Current	Unstarted Tasks
	Task Starting Soon
	Tasks In Progress
	Completed Tasks
	Should Have Started Tasks
	Slipping Tasks
Costs	Cash Flow
	Budget
	Overbudget Tasks
	Overbudget Resources
	Earned Value
Assignments	Who Does What
	Who Does What When
	To-do List
	Overallocated Resources
Workload	Task Usage
	Resource Usage

LET ME TRY IT

Follow these steps to generate and print one of these basic reports:

1. On the **Project** tab, in the **Reports** group, click **Reports**.

2. Click the category that contains the report you want to generate and then click **Select**.

Basic reports that you have created are listed under the **Custom** category.

3. Click the name of the report you want to generate and then click **Select**.

4. Click **Print** to print the selected report.

If the basic reports included with Project 2010 don't contain the information you need and you don't have the option (or don't want) to use visual reports, you can create your own basic report. The steps for creating a custom basic report are different, depending on what kind of report you are creating.

LET ME TRY IT

To create a custom basic task or resource report, follow these steps:

1. On the **Project** tab, in the **Reports** group, click **Reports**.

2. Click **Custom** and then click **Select**.

3. On the **Custom Reports** dialog box, click **New**.

4. Click **Task** or **Resource** in the **Report type** box and then click **OK**.

5. On the **Definition** tab, complete the following:

    - **Name**—Type the name of the report you are creating.
    - **Period**—Choose the time period you want to display in the report.
    - **Count**—Type the number of time periods you want to include in the report. For example, if you chose **Weeks** from the **Period** list, and you type **2** in the **Count** box, the report will display two weeks' worth of data.
    - **Table**—Choose which table type you want to display in the report.
    - **Filter**—Choose how you want to filter the task or resource data.
    - **Highlight**—Select this check box if you want to highlight the filtered tasks in the report.

- **Show summary tasks**—Select this check box to include summary tasks in your report.
- **Gray bands**—Select this check box to include gray lines to divide data visually in your report.

6. On the **Details** tab (shown in Figure 8.4), choose the check boxes for the data you want to include in your report and select or clear the **Border around details, Gridlines between details**, and **Show totals** check boxes to adjust the formatting for your report.

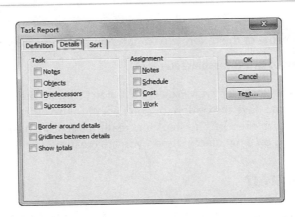

Figure 8.4   *The Details tab of the Task Report dialog box has data and formatting options.*

7. On the **Sort** tab (shown in Figure 8.5), use the **Sort by** and **Then by** lists with the **Ascending** or **Descending** option to choose the order in which data in your report should be listed.

8. Click **OK** to finish creating your custom report.

Follow these steps to create a custom basic monthly calendar report:

1. On the **Project** tab, in the **Reports** group, click **Reports**.

2. Click **Custom** and then click **Select**.

3. On the **Custom Reports** dialog box, click **New**.

4. Click **Monthly Calendar** in the **Report type** box and then click **OK**.

5. Type a name for the new report in the **Name** box.

6. Click **Filter** and choose what data you want to appear in the report.

7. Select the **Highlight** check box if you want to highlight the filtered tasks in the report.

8. Click **Calendar** and choose which calendar you want to use in the report.

9. Select or clear the **Gray nonworking days**, **Solid bar breaks**, and **Print gray bands** check boxes to control how the report displays the calendar.

10. Under **Show tasks as**, choose whether you want the tasks in the report to display as **Bars**, **Lines**, or **Start/Finish dates**.

11. Under **Label tasks with**, select or clear the **ID**, **Name**, and **Duration** check boxes to control what information is displayed for the task in the report.

12. Click **OK** to finish creating your custom report.

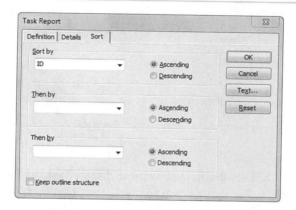

Figure 8.5   *The Sort tab of the Task Report dialog box has options for ordering data.*

Crosstab reports include task and resource information spread across a certain number of time periods.

 LET ME TRY IT

To create a custom basic crosstab report, follow these steps:

1. On the **Project** tab, in the **Reports** group, click **Reports**.

2. Click **Custom** and then click **Select**.

3. On the **Custom Reports** dialog box, click **New**.

4. Click **Crosstab** in the **Report type** box and then click **OK**.

5. On the **Definition** tab, type a name for the new report in the **Name** box.

6. Under **Crosstab**, complete the following:

    - **Column**—Type the number of time periods you want to include, and then choose which time period you are using. For example, type **4** and then choose **Weeks**. Figure 8.6 shows the column options.

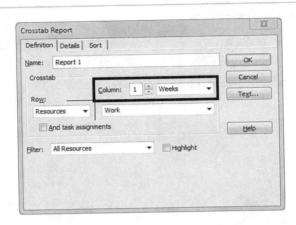

Figure 8.6   *Column options on the Definition tab are highlighted.*

    - **Row**—Choose whether you want to display **Tasks** or **Resources** in each row and then choose which field you want to display across the time period columns. Figure 8.7 shows the row options.

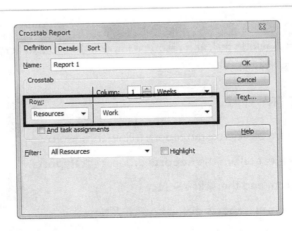

Figure 8.7   *Row options on the Definition tab are highlighted.*

- **And resource assignments/And task assignments**—Select this check box to include assignment information in the report. If you selected **Resources** in the **Row** list, this check box is labeled **And task assignments**. If you selected **Tasks** in the **Row** list, this check box is labeled **And resource assignments**.

7. Click **Filter** and then choose what data you want to appear in the report.

8. Select the **Highlight** check box if you want to highlight the filtered tasks in the report.

9. On the **Details** tab, choose the check boxes for data you want to include in your report and then choose from the following options:

   - **Show zero values**—Select this check box if you want to display a zero when no data has been entered.

   - **Repeat first column on every page**—Select this check box to display the row headers on each page of the report.

   - **Date format**—Choose the format you want to use for dates in your report.

10. On the **Sort** tab, use the **Sort by** and **Then by** lists with the **Ascending** or **Descending** option to choose the order in which data in your report should be listed.

11. Click **OK** to finish creating your custom report.

Sharing Data with Others

So let's say someone else has requested detailed data about your project. Arguably the easiest route in this case is to simply send a copy of the file to the other person and have that person open it with Project 2010 on his or her machine. Unfortunately, it's rarely that easy. If the person requesting information doesn't have Project 2010 installed, your options become a little less direct, but not necessarily less detailed.

Depending on what the other person wants to do with the project data, a few different options are available, as covered in the following sections.

LET ME TRY IT

Copying the Timeline

The timeline is new to Project 2010 and provides a highly visual way to share project information. After setting the timeline up with the information you want to share, you can easily copy it for pasting in another application.

> For more information on using the timeline, see "Using the Timeline" in Chapter 2, "Navigating Project 2010."

Follow these steps to copy the timeline:

1. If the timeline is not currently displayed, on the **View** tab, in the **Split View** group, select the **Timeline** check box, as shown in Figure 8.8.

Figure 8.8   *The Timeline check box is on the View tab, in the Split View group.*

2. Click once in the **Timeline** portion of the Project window to select it.

3. On the **Format** tab, in the **Copy** group, click **Copy Timeline** and then choose whether you're copying it **For E-mail**, **For Presentation**, or **Full Size**. Project will use different formatting options based on your selection.

With the timeline copied to the Clipboard, open the e-mail message, presentation deck, or other file where you want to include the project information, and then paste the copied timeline. It will be pasted as an image within the e-mail message or file.

LET ME TRY IT

Exporting Data to Excel

If the person requesting project data wants to be able to actually work with the data itself, the right solution might be to export the data as an Excel workbook.

To export project data to Excel, follow these steps:

1. On the **File** tab, click **Save As**.

2. Browse to the location where you want to save the Excel file.

3. Type a name for the file in the **File name** box.

4. Click **Save as type** and then choose **Excel Workbook**.

> If the person requesting project data is using an older version of Excel, choose Excel 97-2003. You can also choose to save the data as tab-delimited text, comma-delimited text (CSV), or XML.

5. Click **Save**.

6. Follow the steps in the Export Wizard to save the project data.

 LET ME TRY IT

Taking a Picture of Your Project Data

If the person requesting project data just wants to look at the data, not actually do anything with it, you can copy a picture of your project data and share it by pasting it into another file or e-mail message.

Follow these steps to copy a picture of your project data:

1. Format the data in a view the way you want to share it and then select the data you want to share. If you want to share all of the data in the view, you don't need to select any data, just click once anywhere in the view to select it.

2. On the **Task** tab, in the **Clipboard** group, click the arrow on **Copy** and then click **Copy Picture**, as shown in Figure 8.9.

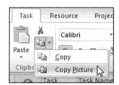

Figure 8.9   *Click the arrow on the Copy button and then click Copy Picture.*

3. Under **Render image**, choose whether you want to copy the image **For screen, For printer**, or **To GIF image file**. If you choose **To GIF image file**, click **Browse** to locate where you want to save the GIF file.

4. Under **Copy**, click **Rows on screen** to copy all of the rows displayed on the screen, or click **Selected rows** to copy only the rows you selected before you clicked **Copy Picture**.

5. Under **Timescale**, click **As shown on screen** to use the full timescale currently displayed in the view, or choose **From** and **To** dates to specify a time period to include.

6. Click **OK** to copy a picture of the project data in the view using the options you selected.

Saving the Project As a PDF or XPS File

Another option for simply viewing project data is to save the project as a PDF or XPS file.

To save the project as a PDF or XPS file, follow these steps:

1. Format the data in a view the way you want to share it and then, on the **File** tab, click **Save As**.

2. Browse to the location where you want to save the PDF or XPS file.

3. Type a name for the file in the **File name** box.

4. Click **Save as type** and then choose **PDF Files** or **XPS Files**.

5. Click **Save**.

6. On the **Document Export Options** dialog box, under **Publish Range**, click **All** to include the entire project or click **From** and specify a date range to only include a certain time period.

7. Under **Include Non-Printing Information**, select or clear the **Document Properties** and **Document Showing Markup** check boxes to choose which options to include.

8. Under **PDF Options**, select or clear the **ISO 19005-1 compliant (PDF/A)** check box to determine whether the PDF should conform to long-term archiving standards.

9. Click **OK** to save the PDF or XPS file.

Collaborating with Others on Your Project

If you are using Project Professional 2010 with Project Server, you can work on a project plan with others who may not have access to your Project Server. By saving the project plan for sharing, you associate the file with its checked-out location in Project Server. The file then can be sent around to others, who can use Project Professional 2010 on their own machines to make changes. Then, when the file is returned to you with changes, you can open it up and check it back in to Project Server.

 SHOW ME   Media 8.2—Collaborating on a Project
Access this video file through your registered Web Edition at
my.safaribooksonline.com/9780132182461/media.

 LET ME TRY IT

To save a project for sharing with others, follow these steps:

1. With Project Professional 2010 opened and connected to Project Server, click the **File** tab and then click **Open**.

2. Click **Retrieve the list of all projects from Project Server** and then double-click the name of the file you want to share with others.

3. On the **File** tab, click **Save Project as File**.

4. Click **Save for Sharing** and then click **Save As**.

5. Type a name for the project file in the **File name** box. A best practice here is to use the same name as the Project Server filename.

6. Locate where you want to save the file locally and then click **Save**.

With the file saved locally, you can attach it to e-mail or place it on a network share to enable others to open it. Other people opening this file must also have Project Professional 2010. Although the file is saved locally, it remains checked out from Project Server. When changes are made to the file, you can check it back in to Project Server.

LET ME TRY IT

Follow these steps to check the file back in to Project Server, with changes:

1. With Project Professional 2010 opened and connected to the same Project Server on which the project is checked out, click the **File** tab and then click **Open**.

2. Locate the changed, shared file, and then click **Open**.

3. On the **File** tab, click **Save As**.

4. Click the name of the file in the **Save to Project Server** box.

5. Click **Save** to replace the file on the server with the file you were sharing.

This chapter covers how to customize fields, views, and tables in Project 2010.

9

Customizing Project 2010

There are many ways to customize Project 2010 to meet your organization's needs. Among the more common ways are custom fields, custom tables, and custom views. By customizing these three elements, you'll be able to capture exactly the information you need and display it in just the way you want using the framework provided by Project 2010.

 TELL ME MORE   Media 9.1—Benefits of Customizing Project 2010
Access this audio recording through your registered web edition at
my.safaribooksonline.com/9780132182461/media.

Creating Custom Fields

Custom fields can be used to add information to your project that isn't captured using the default fields that come with Project 2010. That information might be specific to your project, your team, or your organization, for example.

 SHOW ME   Media 9.2—Create a Custom Field
Access this video file through your registered Web Edition at
my.safaribooksonline.com/9780132182461/media.

 LET ME TRY IT

To create a custom field in your project, follow these steps:

1. On the **Project** tab, in the **Properties** group, click **Custom Fields**.

2. Choose whether you are customizing a **Task** or **Resource** field, as shown in Figure 9.1.

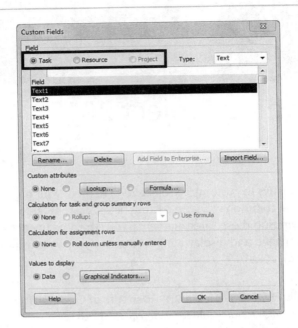

Figure 9.1 *Choose from Task, Resource, or Project in the highlighted portion of the Custom Fields dialog box.*

If you are connected to Project Server, you can also customize project fields using Project Web App.

3. In the **Type** list, click the type of data you plan to enter in the field you are customizing.

4. In the **Field** box, click the name of the field you are customizing. If the field has a friendly name followed by the original, generic name in parentheses, it is most likely already being used.

5. Click **Rename**, type a new friendly name for the field in the **New name for** box, and then click **OK**.

6. Under **Custom Attributes**, if you just want to be able to enter data in the field, leave it set to **None**. However, if you want to control the data, choose one of the following options:

   - **Lookup**—If you want to choose a value from a list, click **Lookup**, type each of the list values in the **Value** column, choose any other options that may make sense for your list, and then click **Close**.

- **Formula**—If you want to calculate the value in the field using dates or other project data, click **Formula**. Formulas can only be used to calculate data for a single task or resource. Formulas cannot reference the values of fields in other tasks or resources. For example, if you create a formula that displays or acts upon the **Start Date** field, that formula will only be using the start date for the corresponding task.

> Office.com has a great resource to help you build your own formulas. "Project functions for custom fields" is available at http://office.microsoft.com/project-help/HP010080956.aspx. It provides a list of functions, including descriptions and examples, that you can use within formulas for custom fields in Project 2010.

7. Under **Calculation for task and group summary rows**, choose one of the following options:

    - **None**—Click **None** if you don't want the field rolled up to the task and group summary levels.

    - **Rollup**—Click **Rollup** and choose how you want the rollup calculated if you want the field values summarized at the task and group summary levels.

    - **Use formula**—Click **Use formula** if you selected **Formula** under **Custom attributes** and you want to use that formula for the rollup values for the field you're customizing.

8. Under **Calculation for assignment rows**, click **None** if you don't want the values in this custom field to be spread across assignments or click **Roll down unless manually entered** if you want the values spread evenly across each assignment. If you choose **Roll down unless manually entered**, the values will be evenly distributed, but you'll still be able to manually enter data to refine the distribution.

9. Under **Values to display**, click **Data** to display the data "as is" or click **Graphical Indicators** to display an icon based on the data entered in the field. For example, you can assign red, yellow, and green icons to different status descriptors to provide a visual health indicator.

10. Click **OK** to save your custom field.

SHOW ME   Media 9.3—Graphical Indicators
Access this video file through your registered Web Edition at
my.safaribooksonline.com/9780132182461/media.

After you've customized a field, you can add it as a column in a view.

Adding and Removing Columns in a View

The process of adding and removing columns in views in Project 2010 is incredibly easy. However, the concept behind what happens sometimes can be confusing, so before we get into how to add and remove columns, let's talk a bit about what's going on behind the scenes.

It's important to remember that behind the shiny interface of Project 2010, there's a database. A nice, stable, giant database. When you use Project to add information about your project, that information makes its way into that database. In the Project interface, you use views to look at the data in that database, as illustrated in Figure 9.2. Views are set up to slice and dice the information in the database, in a way that helps make sense of it. Columns are just parts of views. They're a way of surfacing specific parts of the database.

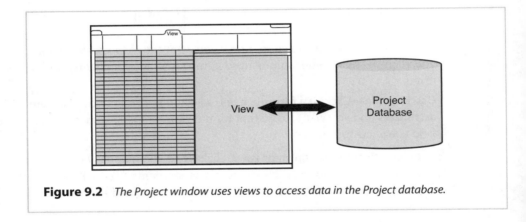

Figure 9.2   *The Project window uses views to access data in the Project database.*

The confusion around this often comes when you go to remove a column from a view. Let's say you've had a column in a view for a long time and data has been added to the column. You decide you no longer need that data, so you hide the column in the view. Then later, you decide you want to use that column for another purpose, so you add it again, and lo and behold your data is still in there. This sometimes comes as a rude surprise to some Project users, who thought that by hiding the column, the data would go away.

When you hide a column, that's really all you're doing. You're taking that way of viewing information in the database out of a view. Imagine if you were simply trying to change which view surfaced the information. Let's say you had a column of information in one view, and after you had been using it for a while, you realized it would be better suited for another view. If you had to re-create the column with its data in another view, it could really become quite an effort if you had a large project with several hundred rows of data.

So if columns are just a way to surface information in the database, how do you remove the data from the database altogether? Select the cells in a column that contain the data you want to delete and then press **Delete**. Got a lot of rows? Click the first cell in the column, scroll to the last row in the table, press and hold **Shift**, click the last cell in the column, and then press **Delete**. Poof, your data is gone.

> This might be a good time to point out that Project supports multiple undo levels. That is, you can undo things you did several actions ago by clicking **Undo** or pressing **Ctrl+Z** multiple times. You can set how many undo levels you want to support on a project. On the **File** tab, click **Options**. Click **Advanced**. Under **General**, type the number of undo levels you want to support in the **Undo levels** box and then click **OK**.

Adding a Column to a View

In any view with data displayed in a table, such as the Gantt Chart view, simply scroll to the right side of the table portion of the view and you'll see the Add New Column header, as shown in Figure 9.3.

Figure 9.3   *Click Add New Column to add a column to the current view.*

To add a new column, click that header and then click the name of the column you want to add. After the column is added, you can click and drag it to relocate it within the view. Click the new column header to select the column and then use the four-direction arrow cursor to drag and drop the column within the view.

Alternatively, you can add a column exactly where you want it to appear. Right-click the column header for the column that you want to appear to the right of the column you're adding and then click **Insert Column**. Click the name of the column to add it to the view.

Not sure what field you want to add? A field reference guide is available on Office.com and provides descriptions of each default field included in Project 2010. To use this guide, visit http://office.microsoft.com/project-help/HA010370279.aspx.

Hiding a Column in a View

If you want to remove a column from a view without removing the data, click the column header to select the column and then press **Delete**. Alternatively, you can right-click the column header and then click **Hide Column**, as shown in Figure 9.4.

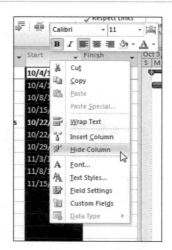

Figure 9.4   *Right-click a column header and then click Hide Column.*

With either of these options, the data that was entered in that column is not removed from your project. I really can't emphasize this enough. If you want to remove the data, select the cells containing the data and then press **Delete**. You'll see the data in the cells is no longer there after you press **Delete**. If you don't actually see the data gone from the cells in the column, there's a good chance it's still sitting back there in the database. Consider this fair warning!

Saving a Set of Columns as a Table

The set of columns within a view is called a *table*. For views that contain tables, you can choose from a list of tables to determine what data is displayed. On the **View** tab, in the **Data** group, click **Table** to see the list of available tables for that view. If the existing tables don't meet your needs, you can create a new table that will be available for use in all task views or all resource views.

There are two ways to create a new table. If you have customized a table in a view by adding or removing columns and you want to save that table as is, on the **View** tab, in the **Data** group, click **Tables** and then click **Save Fields as a New Table**. Type a name for the new table and then click **OK**.

 SHOW ME   Media 9.4—Create a New Table
Access this video file through your registered Web Edition at
my.safaribooksonline.com/9780132182461/media.

 LET ME TRY IT

To create a new table from scratch, follow these steps:

1. On the **View** tab, in the **Data** group, click **Tables** and then click **More Tables**.

2. Click **Task** or **Resource**, depending on what data you're including in the new table, as shown in Figure 9.5.

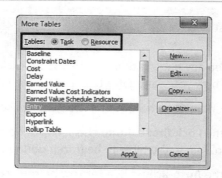

Figure 9.5   *Choose whether to include Task or Resource data.*

3. Click **New** and then type a name for your new table in the **Name** box.

4. Select the **Show in menu** check box, to the right of the **Name** box (as shown in Figure 9.6), if you plan on using the new table frequently. If you select this check box, the new table is included in the list that appears when you click **Tables** on the ribbon.

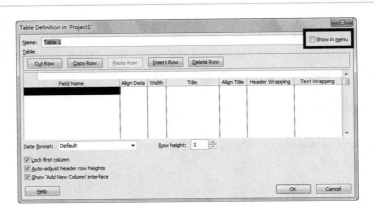

Figure 9.6   *The Show in menu check box appears to the right of the Name box.*

5. Under **Table**, choose which fields you want to include in the table as columns by filling out the **Field Name, Align Data, Width, Title, Align Title, Header Wrapping**, and **Text Wrapping** columns.

You can use the **Cut Row, Copy Row, Paste Row, Insert Row**, and **Delete Row** buttons to edit the list of fields.

6. If you've included any date fields in the new table, click the **Date format** list and choose how you want dates to appear in the table.

7. Type a number in the **Row height** box to adjust row spacing.

8. Select or clear the **Lock first column** check box to determine whether you want the first column in the table to be frozen during scrolling.

9. Select or clear the **Auto-adjust header row heights** check box to let Project automatically increase or decrease the height of the header row, based on header text length.

10. Select or clear the **Show 'Add New Column' interface** check box to deter-mine whether you want to include the ability to add new columns to the table using the far-right column, labeled **Add New Column**.

11. Click **OK** to create the new table.

If you selected the **Show in menu** check box to display the table, on the **View** tab, in the **Data** group, click **Tables** and then click the name of the new table.

If you did not select the **Show in menu** check box to display the table, on the **View** tab, in the **Data** group, click **Tables** and then click **More Tables**. Click **Task** or **Resource**, depending on which type of table you created. Click the name of the new table and then click **Apply**.

Creating and Editing Views

If the default views in Project 2010 don't meet your needs, you can make changes to an existing view or create your own by choosing different display elements, such as a table, a group, or a screen. You can create or edit a single view (in which one view is displayed in the Project window) or a combination view (in which two views are displayed in the Project window at one time).

 SHOW ME   Media 9.5—Create a New View
Access this video file through your registered Web Edition at
my.safaribooksonline.com/9780132182461/media.

 LET ME TRY IT

Follow these steps to create or edit a single view:

1. On the **View** tab, in the **Task Views** or **Resource Views** group, click **Other Views** and then click **More Views**.

2. If you are editing an existing view, click the name of the view in the list (as shown in Figure 9.7) and then click **Edit**. If you are creating a new view, click **New**.

3. If you are creating a new view, on the **Define New View** dialog box, click **Single view** and then click **OK**. If you are editing an existing view, skip this step.

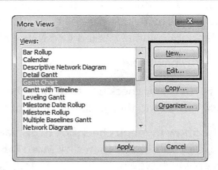

Figure 9.7 *Click New, or select a view and click Edit.*

4. On the **View Definition** dialog box, edit the following fields:

   • **Name**—Type a name for the view.

   • **Screen**—Choose what type of view you are creating. If you are editing an existing view, this option cannot be changed.

   • **Table**—Choose what table you want to display in the view, if the view type you selected includes a table.

   • **Group**—Choose how you want to group data in the view, if the view type you selected includes grouping. If you don't want to group data, click **No Group** in the list.

   • **Filter**—Choose how you want to filter data in the view, if the view type you selected includes filtering. If you don't want to filter data, click **All Tasks** or **All Resources** in the list.

   • **Highlight filter**—Select this check box to highlight the filtered data, instead of hiding data that doesn't meet the filter criteria.

   • **Show in menu**—Select this check box to include the view in the corresponding menu on the **View** tab. For example, if the view type (**Screen**) is **Gantt Chart**, the view will appear in the list when you click **Gantt Chart** on the **View** tab.

Customizations made to individual views are specific to those views. This includes bar and box styles, as well as usage view data fields. For example, if you customize the way Gantt bars appear in one view, when you create a new view or go to another view that contains Gantt bars, the customizations will not persist. You'll need to customize the Gantt bars in that view, as well, if you want them to appear the same.

5. Click **OK** to save the view.

LET ME TRY IT

A combination view is a view in which two views are displayed in the Project window at one time. For example, the **Task Entry** view, shown in Figure 9.8, is a combination view. It displays the **Gantt Chart** view on the top portion of the screen, and the **Task Form** view on the bottom portion.

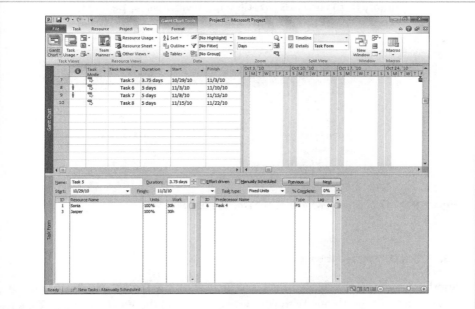

Figure 9.8   *The Task Entry view is a combination view.*

To create or edit a combination view, follow these steps:

1. On the **View** tab, in the **Task Views** or **Resource Views** group, click **Other Views** and then click **More Views**.

2. If you are editing an existing view, click the name of the view in the list and then click **Edit**. If you are creating a new view, click **New**.

3. If you are creating a new view, on the **Define New View** dialog box, click **Combination view** and then click **OK**. If you are editing an existing view, skip this step.

4.   On the **View Definition** dialog box, shown in Figure 9.9, edit the following fields:

*   **Name**—Type a name for the view.

*   **Primary View**—Choose the view you want to display in the top portion of the Project window.

*   **Details Pane**—Choose the view you want to display in the bottom portion of the Project window.

*   **Show in menu**—Select this check box to include the view in the corresponding menu on the **View** tab. For example, if the view type for the primary (top) view is **Gantt Chart**, the view will appear in the list when you click **Gantt Chart** on the **View** tab.

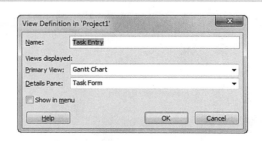

Figure 9.9   *Define the views to include in the combination view.*

5.   Click **OK** to save the view.

Another way to save a custom view is to first set up the Project window using the views and tables you want. With your views set up, on the **View** tab, in the **Task Views** or **Resource Views** group, click **Other Group** and then click **Save View**. Type a name for the new view and then click **OK**.

This chapter explains the various options available to control aspects of your project.

10

Understanding Project Options

The Project Options dialog box provides several choices for controlling how Project 2010 behaves, as well as how your individual project behaves.

To begin setting the options for your project, click the **File** tab and then click **Options**, as shown in Figure 10.1.

Figure 10.1   *Click File and then click Options.*

The sections in this chapter go through each of the option groupings listed on the left side of the Project Options dialog box, as shown in Figure 10.2.

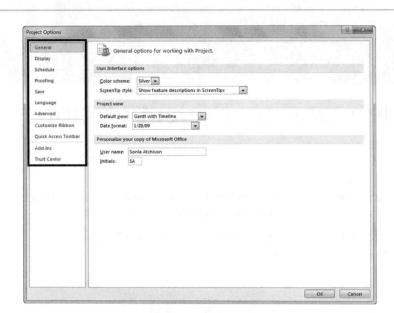

Figure 10.2   *Options are grouped into tabs on the Project Options dialog box.*

General Project Options

The General tab of the Project Options dialog box, as shown in Figure 10.3, includes three sections: User Interface options, Project view, and Personalize your copy of Microsoft Office.

User Interface Options

Options listed under User Interface options on the General tab (shown in Figure 10.4) include Color scheme and ScreenTip style, as described in the following sections.

Color Scheme

Choose from **Blue**, **Silver**, or **Black**. This changes the overall color used to display the Project 2010 window.

ScreenTip Style

ScreenTips are the text that appears when you hover your mouse cursor over various buttons and options within the Project 2010 interface. The ScreenTip style option enables you to choose how you want ScreenTips to behave in Project 2010.

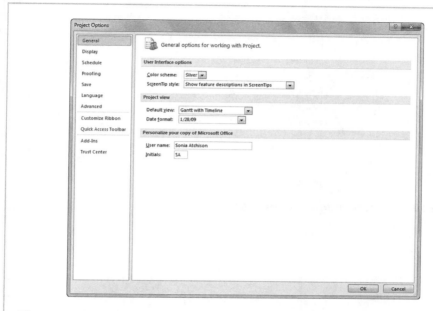

Figure 10.3 *The General tab of the Project Options dialog box*

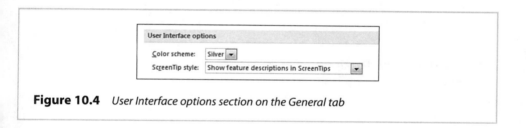

Figure 10.4 *User Interface options section on the General tab*

Choose **Show feature descriptions in ScreenTips** to include text that explains the button or option that you are hovering over, as shown in Figure 10.5.

Choose **Don't show feature descriptions in ScreenTips** to only show the button or option name when hovering over a feature, as shown in Figure 10.6.

Choose **Don't show ScreenTips** to turn ScreenTips off entirely. With this option selected, hovering over a button or option will not pop up any text.

Project View

Options listed under Project view on the General tab (shown in Figure 10.7) include Default view and Date format, as described in the following sections.

Figure 10.5   *ScreenTip with feature description*

Figure 10.6   *ScreenTip without feature description*

Figure 10.7   *Project view section on the General tab*

Default View

The default view is the view that is displayed when you first open a project in Project 2010. If you want the default view to be something other than the Gantt Chart view with the Timeline displayed, select that view from the **Default view** list. The entire list of Project 2010 views, including any custom views you have created, is included in this list.

Date Format

Choose the format you want to use for dates in your project from the **Date format** list.

Personalize Your Copy of Microsoft Office

Options listed under Personalize your copy of Microsoft Office on the General tab (shown in Figure 10.8) include User name and Initials, as described in the following sections.

Figure 10.8   *Personalize your copy of Microsoft Office section on the General tab.*

User Name

If your name, or the name you want to associate with Project files, is different from the name displayed in this box by default, you can change it here. This name will be populated in the properties for the project. You can, however, change or delete it from the Project Properties dialog box if you would rather not include it with this project file.

Initials

If your initials, or the initials that you want to use to indicate changes you have made to the project, are different from the initials displayed in this box by default, you can change them here.

Display Options

The Display tab of the Project Options dialog box, as shown in Figure 10.9, includes four sections: Calendar, Currency options for this project, Show indicators and options buttons for, and Show these elements.

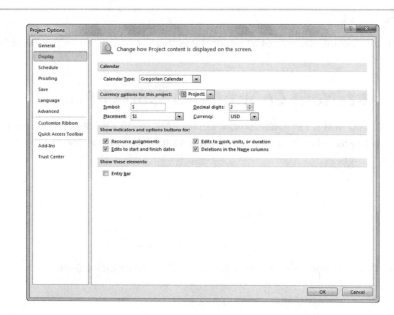

Figure 10.9   *The Display tab of the Project Options dialog box*

Calendar

Under **Calendar**, choose the **Calendar Type** you want to use for your project. You can choose from **Gregorian Calendar**, **Hijri Calendar**, or **Thai Buddhist Calendar**. Figure 10.10 shows the Calendar section.

Figure 10.10   *Calendar section on the Display tab*

Currency Options for This Project

You can choose to apply the options listed under Currency options for this project, on the Display tab (shown in Figure 10.11), to a specific project, as opposed to broadly, for all projects you work with in Project 2010.

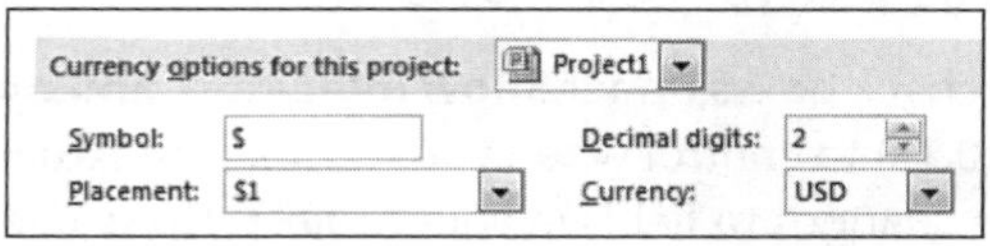

Figure 10.11   *Currency options for this project section on the Display tab*

To choose which project to apply these options to, click the name of the project in the list included in the section header, as shown in Figure 10.12.

Figure 10.12   *Choose which project these options apply to.*

Options listed under Currency options for this project include Symbol, Decimal digits, Placement, and Currency, as described in the following sections.

Symbol

Type the symbol to use for currency values. For example, if your project primarily deals in dollars, type the **$** symbol in this box.

Decimal Digits

Type the number of digits to include after the decimal point in currency values. For example, if you set this value to **2**, a currency value might look like this: $12,345.67.

Placement

Choose where you want the symbol to appear, in relation to the currency number. You can choose to include it to the immediate left or right of the number ($1 or 1$), or include a space between the symbol and the number ($ 1 or 1 $).

Currency

Choose the currency that the project primarily uses. If you have individual values to add to your project that use a currency other than the default you set here, you will need to convert that value before adding it to your project.

Show Indicators and Options Buttons For

Select or clear the check boxes under **Show indicators and options buttons for** (shown in Figure 10.13) to control when you want a contextual menu to appear when you've made changes to fields in your project. These check boxes include **Resource assignments; Edits to work, units, or duration; Edits to start and finish dates**; and **Deletions in the Name columns**.

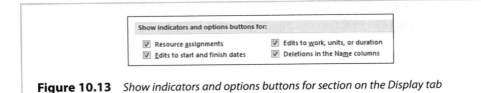

Figure 10.13   *Show indicators and options buttons for section on the Display tab*

The best practice here is to select these check boxes because these messages can be very helpful for any level of Project user.

Show These Elements

Under **Show these elements** (shown in Figure 10.14), select the **Entry bar** check box to add a text entry field above the view where you're entering data, similar to entering data in an Excel spreadsheet.

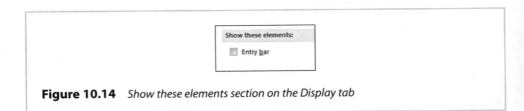

Figure 10.14   *Show these elements section on the Display tab*

Figure 10.15 shows the entry bar in the Gantt Chart view.

Schedule Options

The Schedule tab of the Project Options dialog box, as shown in Figure 10.16, includes six sections: Calendar options for this project, Schedule, Scheduling options for this project, Schedule Alerts Options, Calculation, and Calculation options for this project.

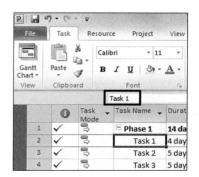

Figure 10.15 *The entry bar is displayed above the grid in a view.*

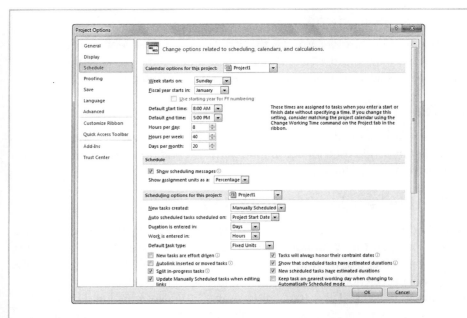

Figure 10.16 *The Schedule tab of the Project Options dialog box.*

Calendar Options for This Project

You can choose to apply the options listed under Calendar options for this project, on the Schedule tab (shown in Figure 10.17), to a specific project. To choose which project to apply these options to, click the name of the project in the list included in the section header.

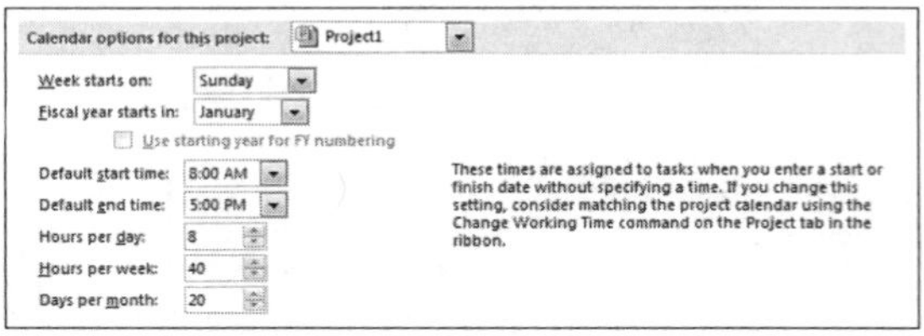

Figure 10.17 *Calendar options for this project section on the Schedule tab.*

Options listed under Calendar options for this project are described in the follow-ing sections.

Week Starts On

Choose the day that begins each week in the selected project. For example, some organizations may consider Monday the first day of the week, whereas other organizations may consider Sunday to be the first day of the week. Setting this option controls how calendars are displayed in the selected project.

Fiscal Year Starts In

Choose the first month of the fiscal year for the selected project. The fiscal year is the 12-month period used for accounting purposes, and may be the same as, or different from, the calendar year.

Use Starting Year for FY Numbering

If you choose any month other than January from the **Fiscal year starts in** list, the **Use starting year for FY numbering** check box becomes available. This is because a fiscal year that begins midway through a calendar year will include some months during the first calendar year and other months during the second calendar year. For example, if my fiscal year starts in November 2011, November and December will be in calendar year 2011, and the rest of my fiscal year (January through October) will be in calendar year 2012.

If you want to use the first calendar year as the year included in fiscal year number-ing, select the **Use starting year for FY numbering** check box. For example, if I select this check box, the numbering for a fiscal year that starts in November 2011 will continue to be FY11, even through the months actually fall in the 2012 calendar year.

Default Start Time

Choose the start time for a typical work day in the selected project. If necessary, you can adjust this start time for specific tasks or resources within the project.

Default End Time

Choose the finish time for a typical work day in the selected project. If necessary, you can adjust this finish time for specific tasks or resources within the project.

Hours Per Day

Type the number of hours that resources in the selected project typically put in during a work day. If necessary, you can adjust the number of work hours for specific tasks or resources within the project.

Hours Per Week

Type the number of hours that resources in the selected project typically put in during a work week.

Days Per Month

Type the number of working days in a month for the selected project.

Schedule

Options listed under Schedule on the Schedule tab (shown in Figure 10.18) include Show scheduling messages and Show assignment units as a, as described in the following sections.

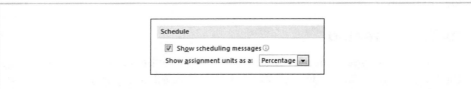

Figure 10.18 *Schedule section on the Schedule tab*

Show Scheduling Messages

Select this check box to display messages, while you work with your project, indicating inconsistencies in your plan. For example, if you change your project so that a successor task starts before a predecessor task has finished, a message will be displayed to alert you of that inconsistency.

Show Assignment Units as A

Choose whether you want to show assignment units as a percentage or a decimal. Assignment units represent how much of a resource's time is currently assigned to a specific task or project.

Scheduling Options for This Project

You can choose to apply the options listed under Scheduling options for this project, on the Schedule tab (shown in Figure 10.19), to a specific project. To choose which project to apply these options to, click the name of the project in the list included in the section header.

Figure 10.19   *Scheduling options for this project section on the Schedule tab*

Options listed under Scheduling options for this project are described in the following sections.

New Tasks Created

Choose whether you want new tasks in your project to be **Auto Scheduled**, using the Project scheduling engine, or **Manually Scheduled**, using only the dates you enter. You can change this setting for each task individually. What you choose here simply sets what the default is for each new task in your project.

Auto Scheduled Tasks Scheduled On

Choose whether you want to use the **Project Start Date** or the **Current Date** as the default start date for new tasks in your project.

Duration Is Entered In

Choose the time units you want to use, by default, when identifying the length of time you think tasks in your project will take (also known as "duration"). You can choose **Minutes, Hours, Days, Weeks,** or **Months.** You can choose any of these time units at any time when entering task durations. Here, you're simply setting what the default is for each new task in your project. Generally, duration is expressed in days.

Work Is Entered In

Choose the time units you want to use, by default, when entering the work completed on tasks in your project. As with duration, you can choose **Minutes, Hours, Days, Weeks,** or **Months,** and you are choosing the default unit for new tasks. Generally, work is expressed in hours, though sometimes days are more appropriate.

Default Task Type

Choose what task type you want to use, by default, for new tasks in your project. You can manually change this on a per-task basis.

New Tasks Are Effort Driven

Select this check box to maintain work values for tasks in your project, by default, as you add or remove assignments. You can manually change this on a per-task basis.

Autolink Inserted or Moved Tasks

Select this check box to automatically link tasks when you insert, delete, or move tasks between existing finish-to-start links. For example, say you have two tasks that are linked, and you right-click the second task to insert another task between them. The inserted task will maintain the link structure, so that it is linked to the task above it as well as the task below it.

Split In-Progress Tasks

Select this check box to allow Project to reschedule remaining duration and work on tasks, as necessary.

Update Manually Scheduled Tasks when Editing Links

Select this check box to include updates to manually scheduled tasks when making changes to links between tasks.

Tasks Will Always Honor Their Constraint Dates

Select this check box to require that Project always maintain constraint dates for tasks in your project.

For example, if a task has a constraint set so that it must start on a specific date, and if the Tasks will always honor their constraint dates check box is selected, you can choose to ignore the links, lag, and lead time between that task and other tasks and maintain the constraint. The task will start on that date, no matter what.

If the Tasks will always honor their constraint dates check box is cleared, the relationship that a task has with other tasks will determine the schedule, even if a constraint is set. So, if a task has a constraint set so that it must start on a specific date, but it's also linked so that it starts after another task, and that other task doesn't finish until after the constraint date, the constraint date will be ignored.

Show That Scheduled Tasks Have Estimated Durations

Select this check box to display a question mark (?) after duration values that are estimated, as opposed to manually entered in the project.

New Scheduled Tasks Have Estimated Durations

Select this check box to initially use estimated durations for tasks in your project. Estimated durations are those that Project has determined, based on other scheduling factors in your plan.

Keep Task on Nearest Working Day when Changing to Automatically Scheduled Mode

Select this check box to align tasks with working days in your calendar when switching those tasks from being manually scheduled to being automatically scheduled. Manually scheduled tasks may be scheduled over nonworking days. When you switch those tasks to automatic scheduling, if this check box is selected, the tasks will be moved to the nearest possible working day.

Schedule Alerts Options

You can choose to apply the options listed under Schedule Alerts Options, on the Schedule tab (shown in Figure 10.20), to a specific project. To choose which project to apply these options to, click the name of the project in the list included in the section header.

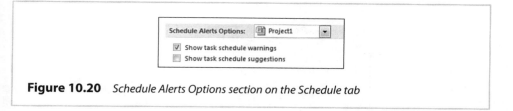

Figure 10.20 *Schedule Alerts Options section on the Schedule tab*

Under **Schedule Alerts Options**, select the **Show task schedule warnings** and/or **Show task schedule suggestions** check boxes to display a warning message and/or suggested options when Project identifies a possible scheduling conflict with a manually scheduled task.

Calculation

Under Calculation, on the Schedule tab (shown in Figure 10.21), choose whether you want Project to recalculate your schedule after every edit.

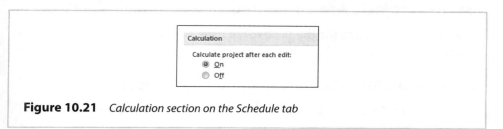

Figure 10.21 *Calculation section on the Schedule tab*

If you choose Off, you will need to manually recalculate your schedule. On the **Project** tab, in the **Schedule** group, click **Calculate Project**. Choosing to turn calculation off is rare, and should only be performed by advanced Project users.

Calculation Options for This Project

You can choose to apply the options listed under Calculation options for this project, on the Schedule tab (shown in Figure 10.22), to a specific project. To choose which project to apply these options to, click the name of the project in the list included in the section header.

Options listed under Calculation options for this project are described in the following sections.

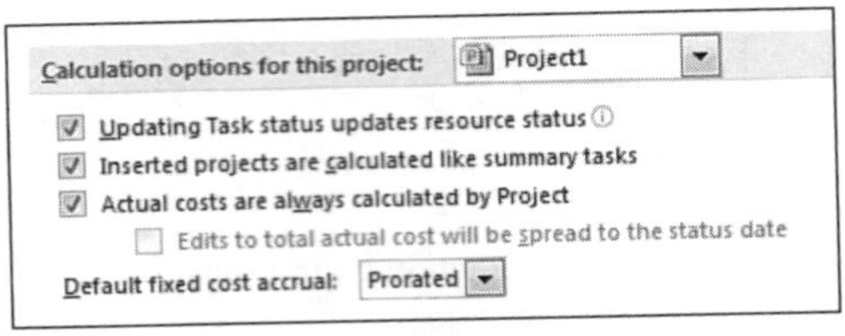

Figure 10.22   *Calculation options for this project section on the Schedule tab*

Updating Task Status Updates Resource Status

Select this check box to automatically update resource assignment status data, such as remaining work, whenever you update task status data, such as percent complete. With this check box selected, updates to assignment status data will also automatically update task status data.

Inserted Projects Are Calculated Like Summary Tasks

Select this check box to use the same rollup rules for inserted projects as are used for summary tasks.

Actual Costs Are Always Calculated by Project

Select this check box to require that actual cost calculation be done only by Project, not manually. If you select this check box, additional actual costs can only be added manually after the task is 100% complete. The best practice here is to leave this check box selected. Clearing it is for advanced users only.

Edits to Total Actual Cost Will Be Spread to the Status Date

Select this check box to evenly distribute actual costs across the project's schedule, to the status date. This check box is only available if the Actual costs are always calculated by Project check box is cleared.

Default Fixed Cost Accrual

Choose whether you want fixed costs to be incurred at the start of a task, at the end of a task, or prorated across the entire duration of a task.

Proofing Options

The Proofing tab of the Project Options dialog box, as shown in Figure 10.23, includes three sections: AutoCorrect options, When correcting spelling in Microsoft Office programs, and When correcting spelling in Project.

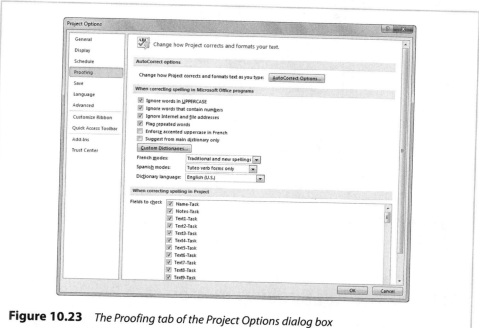

Figure 10.23   *The Proofing tab of the Project Options dialog box*

AutoCorrect Options

Click **AutoCorrect Options**, in the **AutoCorrect Options** section of the **Proofing** tab (shown in Figure 10.24), to change how Project 2010 corrects and formats the text you enter as you plan your project.

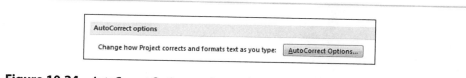

Figure 10.24   *AutoCorrect Options section on the Proofing tab*

When Correcting Spelling in Microsoft Office Programs

Set the options in the **When correcting spelling in Microsoft Office programs** section, on the **Proofing** tab (shown in Figure 10.25), to determine how all Microsoft Office applications (including Project) handle unique spelling issues.

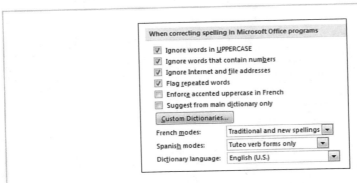

Figure 10.25   *When correcting spelling in Microsoft Office Programs section on the Proofing tab*

When Correcting Spelling in Project

Choose which Project fields to include in spell check by selecting or clearing the check boxes listed under **When correcting spelling in Project**, on the **Proofing** tab (shown in Figure 10.26).

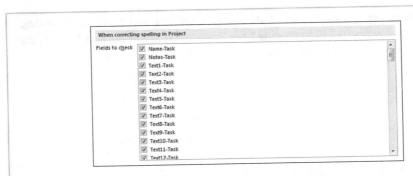

Figure 10.26   *When correcting spelling in Project section on the Proofing tab*

Save Options

The Save tab of the Project Options dialog box, as shown in Figure 10.27, includes three sections: Save projects, Save templates, and Cache.

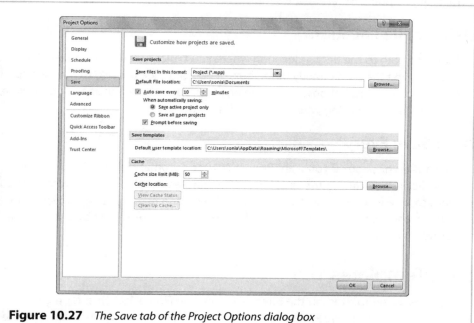

Figure 10.27   *The Save tab of the Project Options dialog box*

Save Projects

Options listed under Save projects on the Save tab (shown in Figure 10.28) include Save files in this format, Default File location, and Auto save every, as described in the following sections.

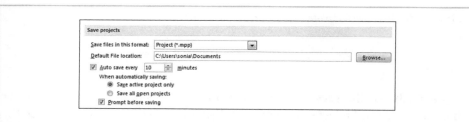

Figure 10.28   *Save projects section on the Save tab*

Save Files in This Format

Choose the default file format for saving project files. You can choose from **Project (*.mpp)**, **Microsoft Project 2007 (*.mpp)**, **Microsoft Project 2000 – 2003 (*.mpp)**, and **Project Template (*.mpt)**. You can choose to save in any of these formats at any point. Here, you are simply choosing which format to use, by default.

Default File Location

Enter the path to the default location where you typically save your project files. You can type the path directly in the box, or you can click **Browse** to navigate to the location. You can choose to save to any appropriate location at any point. Here, you are simply choosing where to save files, by default.

Auto Save Every

Select this check box if you want Project 2010 to automatically save your project periodically. You can set the save interval in minutes and then choose whether you want to save just the project you're currently working in or all open projects, and you can choose whether you want to be prompted before Project saves the corresponding file(s).

Save Templates

Under **Save templates**, on the **Save** tab (shown in Figure 10.29), enter the path where you want to save Project templates (.mpt files), by default. You can type the path to the location, or click **Browse** to navigate to the location. You can choose to save a Project template to another location at any point. Here, you are simply choosing the default location for template files.

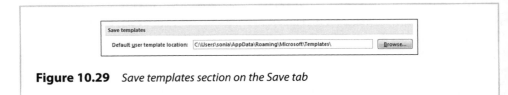

Figure 10.29 *Save templates section on the Save tab*

Cache

Under **Cache**, on the **Save** tab (shown in Figure 10.30), set the size and location for the cache used by Project Professional 2010 when connected to Project Server. This is the portion of your hard drive that is used to save server files locally, making for faster project editing and saving when connected to Project Server.

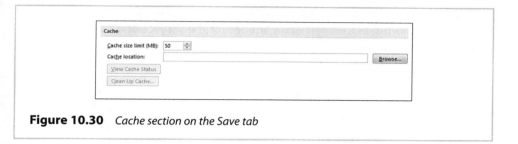

Figure 10.30   *Cache section on the Save tab*

Language Options

The Language tab of the Project Options dialog box, as shown in Figure 10.31, is used to set the editing languages, and display and Help languages, for all Microsoft Office applications, including Project.

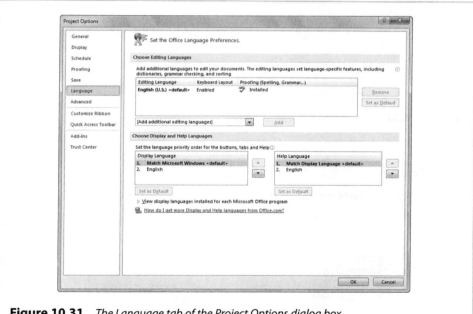

Figure 10.31   *The Language tab of the Project Options dialog box*

Advanced Options

The Advanced tab of the Project Options dialog box, as shown in Figure 10.32, includes 10 sections: General, Project Web App, Planning Wizard, General options for this project, Edit, Display, Display options for this project, Cross project linking options for this project, Earned Value options for this project, and Calculation options for this project.

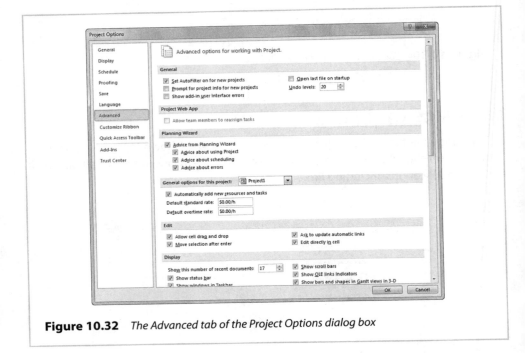

Figure 10.32   *The Advanced tab of the Project Options dialog box*

General

Options listed under General on the Advanced tab (shown in Figure 10.33) are described in the following sections.

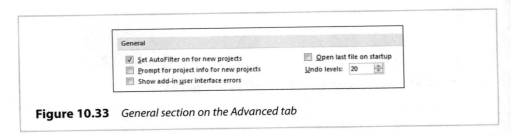

Figure 10.33   *General section on the Advanced tab*

Set AutoFilterOn for New Projects

Select this check box to turn on the ability to filter using column headers, by default. Figure 10.34 shows a column header with AutoFilter turned on.

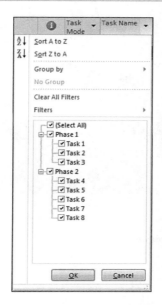

Figure 10.34   *AutoFilter enables you to look for specific data in a column.*

Prompt for Project Info for New Projects

Select this check box to immediately open the Project Information dialog box when creating a new project. Figure 10.35 shows the Project Information dialog box.

Show Add-In User Interface Errors

Select this check box to display error messages when an add-in fails to work properly, in a way that relates to the Project 2010 user interface.

Open Last File on Startup

With this check box selected, when you open Project 2010, the same file that was open when you closed Project will reopen. This can be helpful if you work primarily in one project file at a time.

Undo Levels

Type the number of times you want to be able to click Undo. Consider performance when choosing this number.

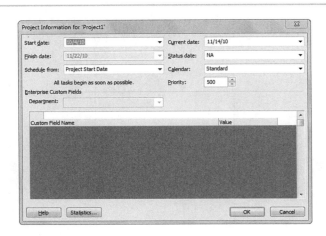

Figure 10.35   *The Project Information dialog box*

Project Web App

If your organization uses Project Professional 2010 with Project Server, select the **Allow team members to reassign tasks** check box, under **Project Web App** on the **Advanced** tab (shown in Figure 10.36), to determine whether resources on a project can reassign their tasks to other resources, using Project Web App.

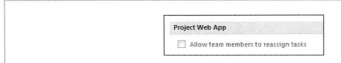

Figure 10.36   *Project Web App section on the Advanced tab*

Planning Wizard

Select the check boxes under **Planning Wizard** on the **Advanced** tab (shown in Figure 10.37) to choose what tips you want to display to help you plan your project. You can choose to display tips about using Project, scheduling, and errors. If you don't want to display any tips, clear the **Advice from Planning Wizard** check box.

General Options for This Project

You can choose to apply the options listed under **General options for this project**, on the **Advanced** tab (shown in Figure 10.38), to a specific project.

To choose which project to apply these options to, click the name of the project in the list included in the section header.

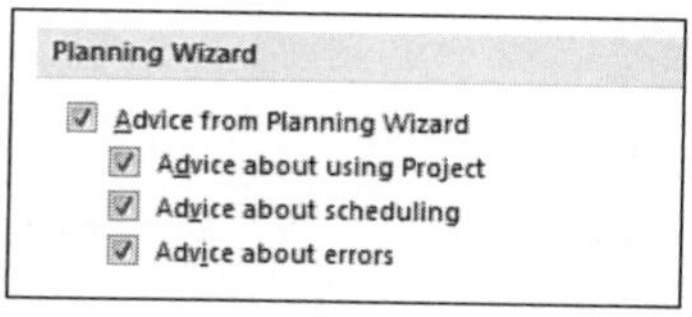

Figure 10.37   *Planning Wizard section on the Advanced tab*

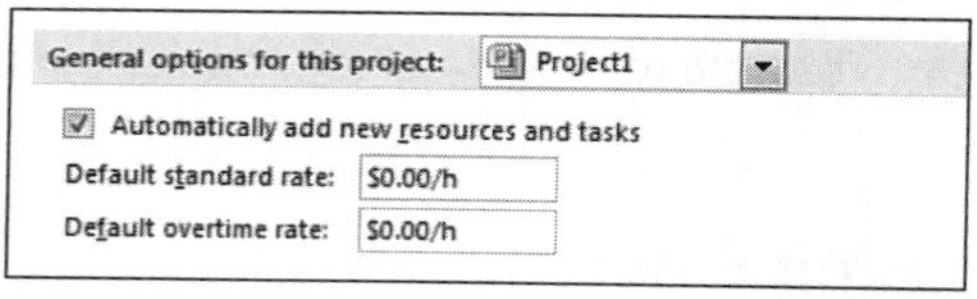

Figure 10.38   *General options for this project section on the Advanced tab*

Options listed under General options for this project are described in the following sections.

Automatically Add New Resources and Tasks

Select this check box to automatically add resources and tasks to the project and resource sheet as you assign work. If this check box is cleared, you will be alerted each time a new resource or task is added to your project through an assignment.

Default Standard Rate

Type a value to use as a standard pay rate for all new resources, by default. This is helpful if many resources use a common pay rate. You can adjust pay rates for individual resources.

Default Overtime Rate

Type a value to use as a default overtime pay rate for new resources. You can adjust overtime rates for individual resources.

Edit

Options listed under Edit on the Advanced tab (shown in Figure 10.39) are described in the following sections.

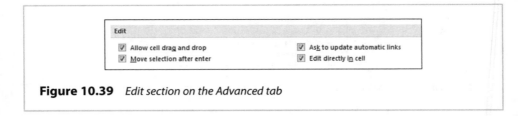

Figure 10.39   *Edit section on the Advanced tab*

Allow Cell Drag and Drop

Select this check box to be able to drag data from one cell or row and drop it in another.

Move Selection After Enter

With this check box selected, pressing **Enter** after typing in a cell moves the cursor to the next row.

Ask to Update Automatic Links

With this check box selected, when you open a project that contains a link to another project, and that other project has been modified, a prompt will ask if you want to update your project with those changes.

Edit Directly in Cell

Select this check box to be able to type directly in cells. If this check box is cleared, be sure to select the **Entry bar** check box on the **Display** tab.

Display

Options listed under Display on the Advanced tab (shown in Figure 10.40) are described in the following sections.

Show This Number of Recent Documents

Under **Display**, type the number of documents you want listed when you click the **File** tab, and then click **Recent**. Figure 10.41 shows the list of recent documents.

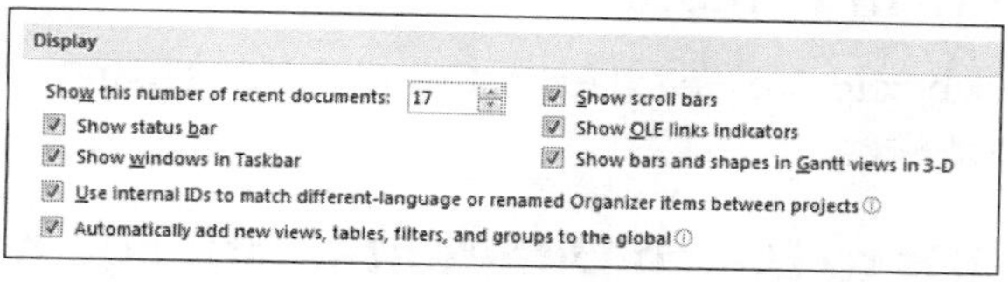

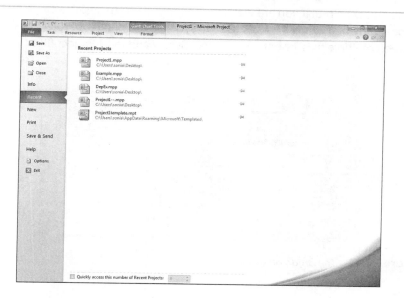

Figure 10.40   *Display section on the Advanced tab*

Figure 10.41   *Recent documents on the File tab*

Show Status Bar

Select this check box to display messages about what Project 2010 is doing, or what actions you might need to take, at the bottom of the Project window. Figure 10.42 shows the status bar.

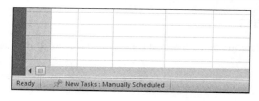

Figure 10.42   *Status bar*

Show Windows in Taskbar

Select this check box to show each Project window as a separate button on the Windows taskbar.

Use Internal IDs to Match Different-Language or Renamed Organizer Items Between Projects

Select this check box to match Organizer elements using internal IDs, instead of words. This is helpful if you are working in multiple languages. The Organizer dialog box, shown in Figure 10.43, is used to synchronize different Project elements between multiple files, or between Project Server and local Project files.

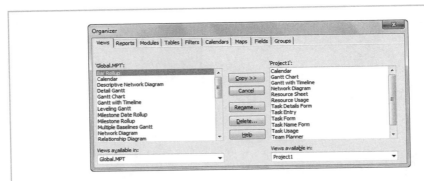

Figure 10.43   *The Organizer dialog box*

To access the Organizer dialog box, click the **File** tab, click **Info**, and then click **Organizer**.

Automatically Add New Views, Tables, Filters, and Groups to the Global

Select this check box to automatically add these items to the global project template, making them available in all projects, instead of just the current project.

Show Scroll Bars

Select this check box to display scroll bars at the far right and bottom of the Project window.

Show OLE Links Indicators

Select this check box to display an indicator for items that are OLE linked within your project. This means that the data in your project is copied from, and linked to, data in another project. Figure 10.44 shows an OLE link indicator.

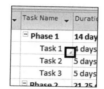

Figure 10.44   *The gray triangle in the bottom right is an OLE indicator.*

Show Bars and Shapes in Gantt Views in 3-D

Select this check box to use 3-D effects on Gantt chart items. If this check box is cleared, flat shapes will be used. Figure 10.45 shows how 3-D Gantt bars compare to flat Gantt bars.

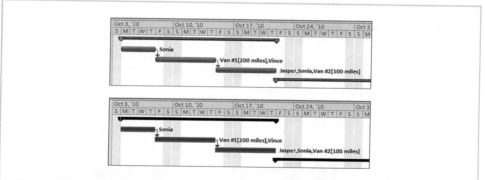

Figure 10.45   *The top set of bars uses 3-D shapes. The bottom set uses flat shapes.*

Display Options for This Project

You can choose to apply the options listed under Display options for this project, on the Advanced tab (shown in Figure 10.46), to a specific project. To choose which project to apply these options to, click the name of the project in the list included in the section header.

Figure 10.46 *Display options for this project section on the Advanced tab*

Options listed under Display options for this project are described in the following sections.

Minutes, Hours, Days, Weeks, Months, and Years

Set the abbreviations you want to use for **Minutes**, **Hours**, **Days**, **Weeks**, **Months**, and **Years**.

Add Space Before Label

Select this check box to insert a space between the number value and the time abbreviation—for example, 1 wk, as opposed to 1wk.

Show Project Summary Task

Select this check box to display a row at the top of your project that summarizes all project data in each column currently displayed. Figure 10.47 shows a project with the project summary task displayed.

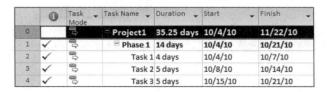

Figure 10.47 *The top row displays the project summary task.*

Underline Hyperlinks

Select this check box to use underlining to visually indicate hyperlinks. Select **Hyperlink color** and **Followed hyperlink color** if you want to use something other than the default blue and purple.

Cross Project Linking Options for This Project

You can choose to apply the options listed under Cross project linking options for this project, on the Advanced tab (shown in Figure 10.48), to a specific project. To choose which project to apply these options to, click the name of the project in the list included in the section header.

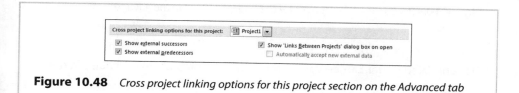

Figure 10.48   *Cross project linking options for this project section on the Advanced tab*

Options listed under Cross project linking options for this project are described in the following sections.

Show External Successors

Select this check box to show tasks from other, linked projects that are successors to tasks in your project.

Show External Predecessors

Select this check box to show tasks from other, linked projects that are predecessors to tasks in your project.

Show 'Links Between Projects' Dialog Box on Open

Select this check box to immediately display the Links Between Projects dialog box when you open a project that contains links to other projects.

Automatically Accept New External Data

Select this check box to automatically add changes to dependencies between tasks in separate projects. This check box is only available when the Show 'Links Between Projects' dialog box on open check box is cleared.

Earned Value Options for This Project

You can choose to apply the options listed under Earned Value options for this project, on the Advanced tab (shown in Figure 10.49), to a specific project. To choose which project to apply these options to, click the name of the project in the list included in the section header.

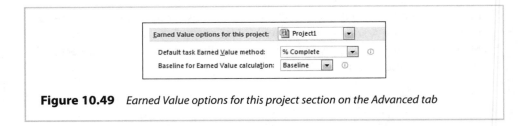

Figure 10.49   *Earned Value options for this project section on the Advanced tab*

Options listed under Earned Value options for this project are described in the following sections.

Default Task Earned Value Method

Choose whether you want to use **% Complete** or **Physical % Complete** for earned value calculations.

Baseline for Earned Value Calculation

Choose which baseline you want to use for analyzing earned value in your project.

Calculation Options for This Project

You can choose to apply the options listed under Calculation options for this project, on the Advanced tab (shown in Figure 10.50), to a specific project. To choose which project to apply these options to, click the name of the project in the list included in the section header.

Options listed under Calculation options for this project are described in the following sections.

Move End of Completed Parts After Status Date Back to Status Date

Select this check box to move actual completed work that was finished prior to the status date, so that the completed portion finishes on the status date. The remainder will continue to be scheduled as planned.

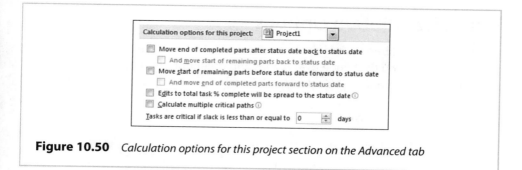

Figure 10.50 *Calculation options for this project section on the Advanced tab*

And Move Start of Remaining Parts Back to Status Date

Select this check box to move the remainder of a task that started early up to start at the status date. This check box is only available if the Move end of completed parts after status date back to status check box is selected.

Move Start of Remaining Parts Before Status Date Forward to Status Date

Select this check box to move remaining work on a task that started late, so that it starts on the status date.

And Move End of Completed Parts Forward to Status Date

Select this check box to move completed work on a task that started late, so that the completed portion finishes on the status date. This check box is only available if the Move start of remaining parts before status date forward to status date check box is selected.

Edits to Total Task % Complete Will Be Spread to the Status Date

Select this check box to evenly distribute changes to total % complete across the schedule to the status date.

Calculate Multiple Critical Paths

Select this check box to calculate the critical path for each set of linked tasks in your project.

Tasks Are Critical if Slack Is Less Than or Equal To

Type a number of days of slack. Tasks with this many, or fewer, days of slack will be identified as critical.

Customize Ribbon Options

The Customize Ribbon tab of the Project Options dialog box, as shown in Figure 10.51, enables you to change the buttons and other options that appear on each of the tabs of the ribbon in Project 2010. You can also create new tabs, new groups, and other options.

Figure 10.51   *The Customize Ribbon tab of the Project Options dialog box*

SHOW ME   Media 10.1—Customizing the Ribbon
*Access this video file through your registered Web Edition at
my.safaribooksonline.com/9780132182461/media.*

LET ME TRY IT

Customize the Ribbon

There are several different ways you can customize the ribbon. The following procedures walk you through adding a command to an existing ribbon tab, creating a new tab, and creating a new group on a tab.

To add a command to an existing tab, follow these steps:

1. Click the **File** tab and then click **Options**.

2. On the **Project Options** dialog box, click the **Customize Ribbon** tab.

3. On the **Customize Ribbon** tab, choose **All Tabs** from the **Customize the Ribbon** list and then expand the name of the tab in the box on the right. Groups on the tab are listed below the tab name.

4. Click the group where you want to add the new command to select it.

5. Under **Choose commands from**, click **All Commands**.

If you know what type of command you want to add to the selected group, choose a command type from the **Choose commands from** list. This will narrow the list of commands, making it easier for you to find what you're looking for.

6. Click the name of the command you want to add to the selected group, and then click **Add** to move it to that group.

7. To reorder the commands within a group, select the command you want to move and then use the up and down arrow buttons to the right of the Customize the Ribbon box to move the selected command up or down in the list.

To create and rename a new tab, follow these steps:

1. Click the **File** tab and then click **Options**.

2. On the **Project Options** dialog box, click the **Customize Ribbon** tab.

3. On the **Customize Ribbon** tab, choose **All Tabs** from the **Customize the Ribbon** list.

4. Click the name of the existing tab that you want to appear just before the new tab. For example, if you want to create a new tab between the **Task** and **Resource** tabs, click the **Task** tab. The new tab will be created after the **Task** tab.

5. Click **New Tab**. A new tab and new group are created.

6. Click **New Tab (Custom)** and then click **Rename**.

7. Type a name for the new tab in the **Display name** box and then click **OK**.

8. Repeat Steps 6 and 7 to rename the new group on the new tab.

To create and rename a new group, follow these steps:

1. Click the **File** tab and then click **Options**.

2. On the **Project Options** dialog box, click the **Customize Ribbon** tab.

3. On the **Customize Ribbon** tab, choose **All Tabs** from the **Customize the Ribbon** list and then expand the name of the tab where you want to create the new group in the box on the right. Groups on the tab are listed below the tab name.

4. Click the name of the existing group that you want to appear just before the new group. For example, if you want to create a new group between the **Insert** and **Properties** groups, click the **Insert** group. The new group will be created after the **Insert** tab.

5. Click **New Group**.

6. Click **New Group (Custom)** and then click **Rename**.

7. Type a name for the new group in the **Display name** box and then click **OK**.

Quick Access Toolbar Options

The Quick Access Toolbar tab of the Project Options dialog box, as shown in Figure 10.52, enables you to choose which options you want to include on the Quick Access toolbar.

The Quick Access toolbar appears at the very top of the Project window, next to the Save, Undo, and Redo buttons. Figure 10.53 shows the Quick Access toolbar.

If you select the **Show Quick Access Toolbar below the Ribbon** check box on the **Quick Access Toolbar** tab, the Quick Access toolbar appears, as shown in Figure 10.54.

 **SHOW ME**   Media 10.2—Customizing the Quick Access Toolbar
Access this video file through your registered Web Edition at
my.safaribooksonline.com/9780132182461/media.

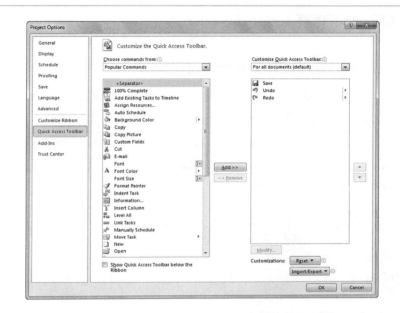

Figure 10.52   *The Quick Access Toolbar tab of the Project Options dialog box*

Figure 10.53   *The Quick Access toolbar appears at the top of the Project window.*

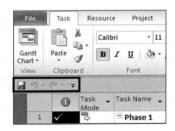

Figure 10.54   *The Quick Access toolbar can also be displayed below the ribbon.*

LET ME TRY IT

Customize the Quick Access Toolbar

To add a command to the Quick Access toolbar, follow these steps:

1. Click the **File** tab and then click **Options**.

2. On the **Project Options** dialog box, click the **Quick Access Toolbar** tab.

3. On the **Quick Access Toolbar** tab, choose **All Commands** from the **Choose commands from** list.

> If you know what type of command you want to add to the Quick Access tool-bar, choose a command type from the **Choose commands from** list. This will narrow the list of commands, making it easier for you to find what you're looking for.

4. Click the name of the command you want to add to the Quick Access tool-bar and then click **Add** to move it to the box on the right.

5. To reorder the commands on the Quick Access toolbar, select the command you want to move from the box on the right, and then use the up and down arrow buttons to the right of the box to move the selected command up or down in the list. This will move the command left or right on the Quick Access toolbar.

Add-Ins Options

The Add-Ins tab of the Project Options dialog box, as shown in Figure 10.55, enables you to manage and view the add-ins used throughout all Microsoft Office applications.

To make changes to your add-ins, at the bottom of the **Add-Ins** tab, choose the add-in type from the **Manage** list and then click **Go**. You can also see a list of dis-abled add-ins. Click **Disabled Items** from the **Manage** list and then click **Go**.

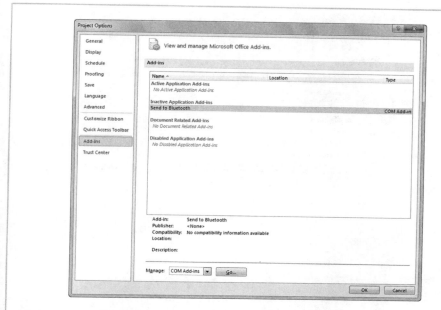

Figure 10.55   *The Add-Ins tab of the Project Options dialog box*

Trust Center Options

The Trust Center tab of the Project Options dialog box, as shown in Figure 10.56, provides information about privacy, security, and the Microsoft Project Trust Center.

Although you are able to modify Trust Center settings on this tab, the best practice is to leave them alone and use the default settings.

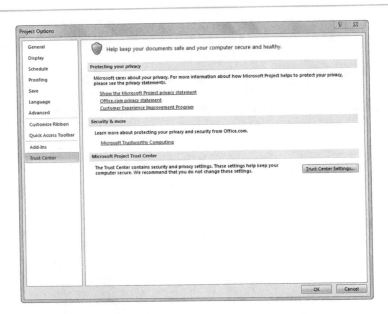

Figure 10.56 *The Trust Center tab of the Project Options dialog box*

This chapter covers how you can use
Project 2010 to resolve common problems
with your project.

11

Dealing with Problems

While managing projects, you will, no doubt, run into any number of problems. This book has provided you with many of the processes for dealing with basic problems, such as splitting tasks and reassigning work to other resources. This chapter covers a few of the more common problem scenarios that we haven't yet dealt with in this book, and how you can use Project 2010 to resolve the issues.

 TELL ME MORE   Media 11.1—Avoiding Future Problems by Using Project 2010 Now

Access this audio file through your registered Web Edition at
my.safaribooksonline.com/9780132182461/media.

Problem: One of My Resources Is Overallocated

Overallocation occurs when a resource in your project is assigned to work that exceeds their available time (the value entered in the resource's **Max Units** field). For example, a resource has a **Max Units** value of 100% for a project. That resource is assigned 75% to one task and 50% to another task at the same time. Because the assignment total is 125%, and the resource's availability is 100%, the resource is overallocated by 25%.

Project 2010 provides a visual indicator when a resource assigned to a task is overallocated. In the **Gantt Chart** view, look for a red icon in the **Indicators** column, as shown in Figure 11.1.

So what do you do if you find that you have overallocated resources in your project? *Resource leveling* is the process of looking at how resources are allocated in your project and moving the assignments around so that tasks are done according to constraints (as soon as possible, for example), but without forcing resources to work beyond 100% of their availability.

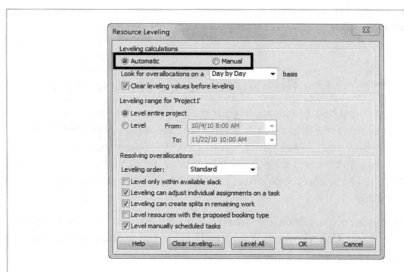

Figure 11.1 *Look for the highlighted red icons in the Indicators column to identify overallocated resources.*

Project 2010 enables you to control how leveling occurs in your project. First, make sure that manual leveling is selected for the project. On the **Resource** tab, in the **Level** group, click **Leveling Options**. On the **Resource Leveling** dialog box, under **Leveling Calculations**, ensure that **Manual** is selected, as shown in Figure 11.2.

Figure 11.2 *Under Leveling Calculations, click Manual.*

SHOW ME   Media 11.2—Manually Leveling Resources
Access this video file through your registered Web Edition at
my.safaribooksonline.com/9780132182461/media.

LET ME TRY IT

You have a few different ways to manually level resources in your project.

To level all resources across all tasks in your project, on the **Resource** tab, in the **Level** group, click **Level All**, as shown in Figure 11.3.

Figure 11.3   *Click Level All to level all resources in your project.*

To level all resources assigned to specific tasks in your project, follow these steps:

1. Press **Ctrl** and click the row header for each task you want to level. This selects the tasks.

2. On the **Resource** tab, in the **Level** group, click **Level Selection**, as shown in Figure 11.4.

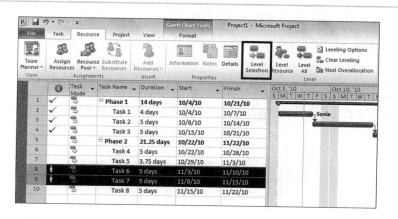

Figure 11.4   *Select the appropriate tasks and then click Level Selection.*

To level specific resource across all tasks in your project, follow these steps:

1. On the **Resource** tab, in the **Level** group, click **Level Resource**, as shown in Figure 11.5.

Figure 11.5   *Select the appropriate tasks and then click Level Selection.*

2. On the **Level Resource** dialog box, shown in Figure 11.6, click the name of the resource you want to level, and then click **Level Now**.

Figure 11.6   *Click the name of a resource, and then click Level Now.*

If, at any point, you no longer want resources leveled on your project, on the **Resource** tab, in the **Level** group, click **Clear Leveling**, as shown in Figure 11.7.

Figure 11.7   *Click Clear Leveling to remove leveling from your project.*

If you have several overallocations that you want to deal with one at a time in a project with many tasks, you can go through the overallocations one at a time by clicking **Next Overallocation** (on the **Resource** tab, in the **Level** group), as shown in Figure 11.8.

Figure 11.8   *Click Next Overallocation to move to the next issue.*

Problem: My Schedule Goes Longer Than My Deadline

It's not uncommon. Resources provided updates to tasks in your project, you just finished adding those updates to your project, and you find that those updates have pushed out the schedule because the work is being completed slower than scheduled. The last task is now scheduled to finish in November, and you have a deadline of the end of October. Or maybe you included a milestone in your project to represent the deadline, and you see that tasks are going beyond that milestone (as shown in Figure 11.9). Any number of expletives may be running through your head, and you're not sure what you should do to pull things back on track.

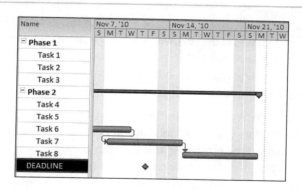

Figure 11.9   *An example of a deadline (indicated by a diamond on the Gantt chart) with tasks in the critical path extending beyond it in the Detail Gantt view*

First things first: You need to figure out what factors are tying your schedule down. You can use the Task Inspector (on the **Task** tab, in the **Tasks** group, click **Inspect**) to help identify which of these factors may be contributing to the lengthy schedule:

- **Constraints**—If tasks in your project have constraints applied, review those constraints and make sure you really need them in place. Does that task really need to start no earlier than that date? Can you make that date a little earlier? Look closely at what you can do to the constraints to save some time in your overall project schedule. For more information on constraints, see Chapter 4, "Working with Tasks."

The constraints that could cause problems in this case would be **Must Start On**, **Must Finish On**, **Start No Earlier Than**, and **Finish No Earlier Than**. These constraints can often cause tasks to be stuck in time and not be able to pull back if one of their predecessors moves back in time.

- **Dependencies**—Look closely at the dependencies you have set up between tasks in your project. Does one task really need to wait for the next task to finish completely, or can it start when the previous task is 50% done? Do those two tasks really need to finish at the same time, or can one finish a bit earlier so that its successor can get started earlier? Make sure that dependencies accurately reflect what needs to happen in your project. See Chapter 4 for more information on overlapping tasks in your project.

- **Durations**—Are the durations of your tasks accurate, or have you added some padding to the durations to give your resources wiggle room? If you padded your durations, now's the time to take that padding out and be realistic about what you need to get done to finish this project on time. This is a very common issue, especially when adding updates from resources to a project. The updates you enter may increase durations, or the actions you take during leveling may push out a finish date. For more information on adjusting task durations, see Chapter 4.

- **Calendars**—This is a tricky one. Remember that you have project, task, and resource calendars to account for. Look at each of these calendars and see how it's affecting the remaining tasks in your project. Is a resource that's assigned to one of the remaining tasks taking a week of vacation in the middle of the task? Can you assign someone else to do the work so that the task can be done sooner? Or can you move the task earlier in the project, before the resource goes on vacation? Evaluate nonworking time in each calendar used by the remaining tasks and see what you can move around to bring in the schedule. For more information on calendars, see the section titled, "Setting Up Your Project's Calendars," in Chapter 3, "Starting a Project."

If adjusting constraints, overlapping tasks, shortening durations, and moving tasks around based on calendar availability doesn't bring your schedule in enough to meet your deadline, you might consider assigning additional resources to your tasks. With more people working on tasks, or more machinery available to do the work, your team may be able to get tasks done more quickly, enabling you to meet your deadline. In thinking about this option, however, it's critical to balance the importance of meeting the deadline with the costs incurred by adding resources to your project. It may make more sense to push the deadline out to a later date. You still incur resource costs because of the additional hours that the existing resources put in past the original deadline, but those costs may be less than the costs incurred by adding more staff or equipment to get the work done on time.

Problem: My Costs Are Exceeding My Budget

You've set a budget for your project, and you've been checking spending against budget regularly, using the processes you learned in Chapter 6, "Accounting for Project Costs." While reviewing costs, you realize that you have now crossed from spending on target to overspending. First, you'll want to figure out where these overages are coming from.

 LET ME TRY IT

To identify the source of cost overages in the Resource Usage view, follow these steps:

1. On the **View** tab, in the **Resource Views** group, click **Resource Usage**.

2. On the **View** tab, in the **Data** group, click **Budget Assignment** in the **Group by** list.

3. On the **View** tab, in the **Data** group, click **Outline** and then click **Outline Level 1**. Each of the groupings collapses so that you can easily look at the numbers for each of the budget assignments.

4. Compare the **Budget Cost** column with the **Actual Cost** column, and the **Budget Work** column with the **Actual Work** column. If the actual values are higher than the budget values, that budget assignment contains overages.

If these columns aren't displayed in the **Resource Usage** view, add them by clicking **Add New Column** on the right side of the table portion of the view. For more information, see the section titled, "Adding Values to Budget Resources," in Chapter 6.

5. Click the plus sign next to the name of the budget assignment that contains the overage. This expands the budget assignment, enabling you to review each resource that has that budget assignment.

6. Look through the actual data for each resource, expanding resource names to see task-specific data. Look across the right pane in the view to see time-phased actual cost and work data.

If the time-phased portion of the view doesn't currently display budget and actual cost and work data, on the **Format** tab, in the **Details** group, click **Add Details**. Use the **Usage Details** tab of the **Detail Styles** dialog box to add these fields to the view.

Also, several visual and basic reports can help you narrow down cost issues, listed in Table 11.1.

Table 11.1   Cost Reports in Project 2010

Excel Reports I	Visio Reports	Basic Reports
Cash Flow	Cash Flow	Cash Flow
Earned Value Over Time		Budget
Resource Cost Summary		Overbudget Tasks
Baseline Cost		
Budget Cost		

For more information on generating reports, see the "Reporting on Your Project" section of Chapter 8, "Sharing Your Project with Others."

After you've identified where the cost issues are occurring, the next step is deciding what you want to do to get your costs back to budget. Baselining may be a good idea here, so that you capture what your data looks like before making modifications. For more information on baselining, see "Baselining Your Project" in Chapter 7, "Capturing Project Progress."

You can take a few approaches to cut back on costs.

Assigning Work to Fewer People

If you've got any extra resources working on your project, perhaps they can be better used on another project. By removing excess resource assignments from your project, you reduce the costs that those resource assignments incur.

> Be careful to only remove extra resources, as overloading the remaining resources can lead to exorbitant and unnecessary overtime pay.

For more information on working with resource assignments, see "Assigning Resources to Tasks" in Chapter 5, "Working with Resources."

Cutting Back on What Needs to Get Done

Are there remaining tasks that aren't 100% necessary for completion of your project? By removing tasks, you also remove resource assignments, thereby reducing the associated costs.

For more information on working with tasks, see Chapter 4.

Trimming Budget Amounts

Are you sure that your budget amounts are accurate? If you've padded your budget a bit for flexibility, now's the time to cinch up the belt and be realistic. Sometimes, all that's needed is a more realistic set of budget data, and your project will be back on track.

For more information on adjusting budget data, see "Adding Values to Budget Resources" in Chapter 6.

index

W

X-Y-Z